YOUR PERSONAL

ASTROLOGY

GUIDE

SAGITTARIUS

2013

YOUR PERSONAL

ASTROLOGY

GUIDE

SAGITTARIUS
2013

RICK LEVINE **& JEFF** JAWER

STERLING ETHOS
New York

STERLING ETHOS
New York

An Imprint of Sterling Publishing
387 Park Avenue South
New York, NY 10016

ISBN 978-1-4027-7962-6

Distributed in Canada by Sterling Publishing
c/o Canadian Manda Group, 165 Dufferin Street
Toronto, Ontario, Canada M6K 3H6
Distributed in the United Kingdom by GMC Distribution Services
Castle Place, 166 High Street, Lewes, East Sussex, England BN7 1XU
Distributed in Australia by Capricorn Link (Australia) Pty. Ltd.
P.O. Box 704, Windsor, NSW 2756, Australia

For information about custom editions, special sales, and premium
and corporate purchases, please contact Sterling Special Sales at
800-805-5489 or specialsales@sterlingpublishing.com.

Manufactured in the United States of America

2 4 6 8 10 9 7 5 3 1

www.sterlingpublishing.com

TABLE OF CONTENTS

Author's Note:

Your Personal Astrology Guide uses the Tropical zodiac based on the seasons, not the constellations. This method of determining signs has been and continues to be the practice of Western astrologers for over 2,000 years. Aries, the beginning of the Tropical zodiac, starts on the first day of spring every year. Contrary to what you may have heard, no one's sign has changed, regardless of when you were born and the addition of a thirteenth sign is not relevant to Western astrology.

Measuring and recording the apparent movement of the Sun, the Moon, and the planets against the backdrop of the heavens is a complex task because nothing is stationary. Even the location of the constellations with respect to the seasons gradually changes from year to year. Since astrologers are concerned with human behavior here on Earth, they created a twelve-fold zodiac that is anchored to four seasons as their primary frame of reference. Obviously, astrologers fully understand that there are eighty-eight official constellations and that the moving planets travel through many of them (including Ophiuchus and Orion), but these are not—and never have been—part of the Tropical zodiac created by astrologers.

THE PURPOSE OF THIS BOOK

The more you learn about yourself, the better able you are to wisely use the energies in your life.
For more than 3,000 years, astrology has been the sharpest tool in the box for describing the human condition. Used by virtually every culture on the planet, astrology continues to serve as a link between individual lives and planetary cycles. We gain valuable insights into personal issues with a birth chart, and can plot the patterns of the year ahead in meaningful ways for individuals as well as groups. You share your sun sign with eight percent of humanity. Clearly, you're not all going to have the same day, even if the basic astrological cycles are the same. Your individual circumstances, the specific factors of your entire birth chart, and your own free will help you write your unique story.

The purpose of this book is to describe the energies of the Sun, Moon, and planets for the year ahead and help you create your future, rather than being a victim of it. We facilitate your journey by showing you the turns ahead in the road of life and hopefully the best ways to navigate them.

YOU ARE THE STAR OF YOUR LIFE

It is not our goal to simply predict events. Rather, we are reporting the planetary energies—the cosmic weather in which you are living—so that you understand these conditions and know how to use them most effectively.

The power, though, isn't in the stars, but in your mind, your heart, and the choices that you make every day. Regardless of how strongly you are buffeted by the winds of change or bored by stagnation, you have many ways to view any situation. Learning about the energies of the Sun, Moon, and planets will both sharpen and widen your perspective, thereby giving you additional choices.

The language of astrology is a gift of awareness, not a rigid set of rules. It works best when blended with common sense, intuition, and self-trust. This is your life, and no one knows how to live it as well as you. Take what you need from this book and leave the rest. Although the planets set the stage for the year ahead, you're the writer, director, and star of your life and you can play the part in whatever way you choose. *Your Personal Astrology Guide* uses information about your sun sign to give you a better understanding of how the planetary waves will wash upon your shore. We each navigate our lives through time, and each moment has unique qualities. Astrology gives us the ability to describe the constantly changing timescape. For example, if you know the trajectory and the speed of an approaching storm, you can choose to delay a leisurely afternoon sail on the bay, thus avoiding an unpleasant situation.

By reading this book, you can improve your ability to align with the cosmic weather, the larger patterns that affect you day to day. You can become more effective by aligning with the cosmos and cocreating the year ahead with a better understanding of the energies around you.

Astrology doesn't provide quick fixes to life's complex issues. It doesn't offer neatly packed black-and-white answers in a world filled with an infinite variety of shapes and colors. It can, however, give you a much clearer picture of the invisible forces influencing your life.

ENERGY & EVENTS

Two sailboats can face the same gale yet travel in opposite directions as a result of how the sails are positioned. Similarly, how you respond to the energy of a particular set of circumstances may be more responsible for your fate than the given situation itself. We delineate the energetic winds for your year ahead, but your attitude shapes the unfolding events, and your responses alter your destiny.

This book emphasizes the positive, not because all is good, but because astrology shows us ways to transform even the power of a storm into beneficial results. Empowerment comes from learning to see the invisible energy patterns that impact the visible landscape as you fill in the details of your story every day on this spinning planet, orbited by the Moon, lit by the Sun, and colored by the nuances of the planets.

You are a unique point in an infinite galaxy of unlimited possibilities, and the choices that you make have consequences. So use this book in a most magical way to consciously improve your life.

MOON CHARTS

2013 NEW MOONS

Each New Moon marks the beginning of a cycle. In general, this is the best time to plant seeds for future growth. Use the days preceeding the New Moon to finish old business prior to starting what comes next. The focused mind can be quite sharp during this phase. Harness the potential of the New Moon by stating your intentions—out loud or in writing—for the weeks ahead. Hold these goals in your mind and help them grow to fruition through conscious actions as the Moon gains light during the following two weeks. In the chart below, the dates and times refer to when the Moon and Sun align in each zodiac sign (see p. 16), initiating a new lunar cycle.

DATE	TIME	SIGN
January 11	2:43 pm EST	Capricorn
February 10	2:20 am EST	Aquarius
March 11	3:51 pm EDT	Pisces
April 10	5:35 am EDT	Aries
May 9	8:28 pm EDT	Taurus (ECLIPSE)
June 8	11:56 am EDT	Gemini
July 8	3:14 am EDT	Cancer
August 6	5:50 pm EDT	Leo
September 5	7:36 am EDT	Virgo
October 4	8:34 pm EDT	Libra
November 3	7:49 am EST	Scorpio (ECLIPSE)
December 2	7:22 pm EST	Sagittarius

2013 FULL MOONS

The Full Moon reflects the light of the Sun as subjective feelings reflect the objective events of the day. Dreams seem bigger; moods feel stronger. Emotional waters run with deeper currents. This is the phase of culmination, a turning point in the energetic cycle. Now it's time to listen to the inner voices. Rather than starting new projects, the two weeks after the Full Moon are when we complete what we can and slow our outward expressions in anticipation of the next New Moon. In this chart, the dates and times refer to when the moon is opposite the sun in each zodiac sign, marking the emotional peak of each lunar cycle.

DATE	TIME	SIGN
January 26	11:38 pm EST	Leo
February 25	3:26 pm EST	Virgo
March 27	5:27 am EDT	Libra
April 25	3:57 pm EDT	Scorpio **(ECLIPSE)**
May 25	12:24 am EDT	Sagittarius
June 23	7:32 am EDT	Capricorn
July 22	2:15 pm EDT	Aquarius
August 20	9:44 pm EDT	Aquarius
September 19	7:12 am EDT	Pisces
October 18	7:37 pm EDT	Aries **(ECLIPSE)**
November 17	10:15 am EST	Taurus
December 17	4:28 am EST	Gemini

ASTROLOGY, YOU & THE WORLD

WELCOME TO YOUR SUN SIGN

The Sun, Moon, and Earth and all the planets lie within a plane called the **ecliptic** and move through a narrow band of stars made up by 12 constellations called the **zodiac**. The Earth revolves around the Sun once a year, but from our point of view, it appears that the Sun moves through each sign of the zodiac for one month. There are 12 months and astrologically there are 12 signs. The astrological months, however, do not match our calendar, and start between the 19th and 23rd of each month. Everyone is born to an astrological month, like being born in a room with a particular perspective of the world. Knowing your sun sign provides useful information about your personality and your future, but for a more detailed astrological analysis, a full birth chart calculation based on your precise date, time, and place of birth is necessary. Get your complete birth chart online at:

http://www.tarot.com/astrology/astroprofile

This book is about your zodiac sign. Your Sun is in optimistic Sagittarius, a fire sign that's hungry for adventure and experience. Playing it safe is not your style, as you're generally more interested in doing things than owning them. This doesn't mean that you can't be materially comfortable; it's simply not the first priority on your list. Relationships are great, too, as long as they don't confine your freedom to express your opinions with total honesty.

THE PLANETS

We refer to the Sun and Moon as planets. Don't worry; we do know about modern astronomy. Although the Sun is really a star and the Moon is a satellite, they are called planets for astrological purposes. The astrological planets are the Sun, the Moon, Mercury, Venus, Mars, Jupiter, Saturn, Chiron, Uranus, Neptune, and Pluto.

Your sun sign is the most obvious astrological placement, for the Sun returns to the same sign every year. But at the same time, the Moon is orbiting the Earth, changing signs every two and a third days. Mercury, Venus, and Mars each move through a sign in a few weeks to a few months.

Jupiter spends a whole year in a sign—and Pluto visits a sign for up to 30 years! The ever-changing positions of the planets alter the energetic terrain through which we travel. The planets are symbols; each has a particular range of meanings. For example, Venus is the goddess of love, but it really symbolizes beauty in a spectrum of experiences. Venus can represent romantic love, sensuality, the arts, or good food. It activates anything that we value, including personal possessions and even money. To our ancestors, the planets actually animated life on Earth. In this way of thinking, every beautiful flower contains the essence of Venus.

Each sign has a natural affinity to an individual planet, and as this planet moves through the sky, it sends messages of particular interest to people born under that sign. Jupiter, your key or ruling planet, shows where you're ready to grow, explore, and push limits in your life. It's the planet of travel, expansion, and the search for meaning that often propels your natural desire to move beyond your comfort zone, widening your experience of the world. Planets can be described by many different words, for the mythology of each is a rich tapestry. In this book we use a variety of words when talking about each planet in order to convey the most applicable meaning. The table below describes a few keywords for each planet, including the Sun and Moon.

PLANET	SYMBOL	KEYWORDS
Sun	☉	Consciousness, Will, Vitality
Moon	☽	Subconscious, Emotions, Habits
Mercury	☿	Communication, Thoughts, Transportation
Venus	♀	Desire, Love, Money, Values
Mars	♂	Action, Physical Energy, Drive
Jupiter	♃	Expansion, Growth, Optimism
Saturn	♄	Contraction, Maturity, Responsibility
Chiron	⚷	Healing, Pain, Subversion
Uranus	♅	Awakening, Unpredictable, Inventive
Neptune	♆	Imagination, Spirituality, Confusion
Pluto	♇	Passion, Intensity, Regeneration

HOUSES

Just as planets move through the signs of the zodiac, they also move through the houses in an individual chart. The 12 houses correspond to the 12 signs, but are individualized, based upon your sign. In this book we use Solar Houses, which place your sun sign in your 1st House. Therefore, when a planet enters a new sign it also enters a new house. If you know your exact time of birth, the rising sign determines the 1st House. You can learn your rising sign by entering your birth date at:

http://www.tarot.com/astrology/astroprofile

HOUSE	SIGN	KEYWORDS
1st House	Aries	Self, Appearance, Personality
2nd House	Taurus	Possessions, Values, Self-Worth
3rd House	Gemini	Communication, Siblings, Short Trips
4th House	Cancer	Home, Family, Roots
5th House	Leo	Love, Romance, Children, Play
6th House	Virgo	Work, Health, Daily Routines
7th House	Libra	Marriage, Relationships, Business Partners
8th House	Scorpio	Intimacy, Transformation, Shared Resources
9th House	Sagittarius	Travel, Higher Education, Philosophy
10th House	Capricorn	Career, Community, Ambition
11th House	Aquarius	Groups and Friends, Associations, Social Ideals
12th House	Pisces	Imagination, Spirituality, Secret Activities

ASPECTS

As the planets move through the sky in their
various cycles, they form ever-changing angles
with one another. Certain angles create significant
geometric shapes. So, when two planets are
90 degrees apart, they conform to a square; 60
degrees of separation conforms to a sextile, or
six-pointed star. Planets create **aspects** when
they're at these special angles. Aspects explain
how the individual symbolism of pairs of planets
combine into an energetic pattern.

ASPECT	DEGREES	KEYWORD
Conjunction	0	Compression, Blending, Focus
Opposition	180	Tension, Awareness, Balance
Trine	120	Harmony, Free-Flowing, Ease
Square	90	Resistance, Stress, Dynamic Conflict
Quintile	72	Creativity, Metaphysical, Magic
Sextile	60	Support, Intelligent, Activating
Quincunx	150	Irritation, Annoyance, Adjustment

2013 GENERAL FORECAST

Astrology works for individuals, groups, and humanity as a whole. You will have your own story in 2013, but it will unfold along with seven billion other tales of human experience. We are each unique, yet our lives touch one another; our destinies are woven together by weather and war, by the economy, science, music, politics, religion, and all the other threads of life on planet Earth.

This astrological look at the major trends and planetary patterns for 2013 provides a framework for comprehending the potentials and challenges we face together, so that we can move forward with tolerance and respect as a community as we also fulfill our potential as individuals.

The astrological events used for this forecast are the transits of major planets Jupiter and Saturn, the retrograde cycles of Mercury, and the eclipses of the Sun and the Moon.

A NOTE ABOUT DATES IN THIS BOOK

All events are based upon the Eastern Time Zone of the United States. Because of local time differences, an event occurring just a few minutes after midnight in the East will actually happen the prior day in the rest of the country. Although the key dates are the exact dates of any particular alignment, some of you are so ready for certain things to happen that you can react to a transit a day or two before it is exact. And sometimes you can be so entrenched in habits or unwilling to change that you may not notice the effects right away. Allow extra time around each key date to feel the impact of any event.

JUPITER IN GEMINI:
LARGER THAN LIFE
June 11, 2012–June 25, 2013

Astrological tradition considers multifaceted Gemini an awkward place for truth-seeking Jupiter. We can be inundated with so much information that it's nearly impossible to see the forest for the trees. Jupiter's long-range vision may be obscured by a million and one ideas that scatter attention, diffusing the focus we need to achieve long-term goals. Yes, this mind-opening transit stirs curiosity about a wide variety of subjects—but it may be difficult to concentrate and gain in-depth knowledge in any one area if we're skimming the surface. Expansive Jupiter in communicative Gemini can also be quite verbose, valuing the volume of information more than its substance. Philosophical flexibility and mental versatility are gifts of this transit, while its less desirable qualities include inconsistency of beliefs and careless planning.

JUPITER IN CANCER:
FEELING IS BELIEVING
June 25, 2013–July 16, 2014

Philosophical Jupiter provides understanding through emotions during its stay in sensitive Cancer. We're likely to reject ideas that do not correspond to gut instincts, applying a subjective check against concepts that sound good but just don't feel right. Returning to traditional sources of wisdom and reconnecting with nature and family deepens our roots in the past to provide a needed sense of stability in these tumultuous times. Yet looking back for answers to today's questions has its limitations; conditions are changing so rapidly now that old rules no longer apply. We gain a sense of safety by relying on time-tested principles, but we may lose the potential for envisioning a creative new tomorrow by following these well-worn paths. The sentimental nature of Jupiter in Cancer favors familiar circles to unfamiliar. Given this transit's protective qualities, this makes it easier to justify closing the door to new people and experiences. Racism, nationalism, and religious and ethnic prejudices are more prevalent when mental gates close to outsiders. Yet Jupiter in nurturing Cancer, at its highest potential, helps us recognize the living nature of truth in an ever-growing spiral that draws upon the best of the old to nourish new goals and aspirations.

SATURN IN SCORPIO:
SHADOWBOXING
October 5, 2012–December 23, 2014
June 14, 2015–September 16, 2015

Responsible Saturn in formidable Scorpio tests our resolve. We are challenged to look into the dark corners of our psyches where fears about love, money, and mortality hide. It's tempting to turn away from these complicated subjects, yet the price of doing so is high because we are then controlled by unconscious impulses. Saturn in Scorpio reminds us that no one is entirely pure and simple. The complexities of giving and receiving affection, dealing with hidden desires, and working with manipulative people are numerous. But if we're willing to show up and do the work, Saturn also offers clarity and authority, enabling us to address these complicated matters. Taking responsibility for dark feelings doesn't mean that we must suppress them; it's a signal to engage them with patience rather than punishment. Personal and professional alliances work more effectively when we stop keeping secrets from ourselves. Finally, with Saturn in Scorpio we could see even more consolidation of financial institutions as a result of bad loans.

MERCURY RETROGRADES
February 23–March 17 in Pisces / June 26–July 20 in Cancer / October 21–November 10 in Scorpio

All true planets appear to move backward from time to time, because we view them from the moving platform of Earth. The most noticeable and regular retrograde periods are those of

Mercury, the communication planet. Occurring three or four times a year for roughly three weeks at a time, these are periods when difficulties with details, travel, communication, and technical matters are more common than usual.

Mercury's retrograde is often perceived as negative, but you can make this cycle work for you. Because personal and commercial interactions are emphasized, you can actually accomplish more than usual, especially if you stay focused on what you need to complete instead of initiating new projects. Still, you may feel as if you're treading water—or worse, being carried backward in an undertow of unfinished business. Worry less about making progress than about the quality of your work. Pay extra attention to all your communication exchanges. Avoiding misunderstandings and omissions is the ideal way to minimize complications. Retrograde Mercury is best used to tie up loose ends as you review, redo, reconsider, and, in general, revisit the past.

All three Mercury retrograde cycles occur in emotional water signs this year. This can make communication more difficult, because it's not easy to translate feelings into words. Our potential loss of objectivity, as well, can lead to even more misunderstandings than usual. Thankfully, these three periods give us the chance to reconnect with our emotions, which can inspire new waves of creativity.

ECLIPSES
Solar: May 9 and November 3
Lunar: April 25, May 25, and October 18

Solar and Lunar Eclipses are special New and Full Moons that indicate significant changes for individuals and groups. They are powerful markers of events, with influences that can appear up to three months in advance and last up to six months afterward.

April 25, Lunar Eclipse in Scorpio: Sink or Swim
This Lunar Eclipse in passionate Scorpio tells us to let go of the past and start living in the present. Taskmaster Saturn's conjunction to the Moon, though, encourages a tenacious attitude that can keep us entangled in unrewarding relationships. Resentment, jealousy, and revenge aren't worth the effort they take to sustain. However, initiating

Mars is conjunct to the sensible Taurus Sun, which favors simplifying life and making a fresh start instead of trying to fix an unresolvable problem.

May 9, Solar Eclipse in Taurus: Trim the Fat
The cost of comfort may become so high that we have to let go of laziness or of some luxuries to make life more affordable. There's a self-indulgent side to Taurus, and with combative Mars and talkative Mercury joined with the Sun and Moon, we can find ourselves aggressively defending our behavior. Yet trying to justify standing still and holding on to what we have may only increase the steep price we pay later for resisting the purging we need now.

May 25, Lunar Eclipse in Sagittarius:
Life's an Adventure
An eclipse in farsighted Sagittarius reminds us to bring our attention back from some distant vision to focus on the here and now. We can discover alternative ways to make life work instead of acting as if there's only one road to fulfillment. Beliefs may not hold up in the face of changing

circumstances that require flexibility instead of certainty. Asking questions reveals options that multiply choices, creating confusion for some but freeing most of us from rigid thinking and excessive judgment.

October 18, Lunar Eclipse in Aries:
No Man Is an Island
Life is not a solo voyage even when we're feeling all alone. This eclipse emphasizes the need to work with others and demands some degree of compromise and accommodation. It's better to sit on the fence, gather more information, and mull things over than to race ahead impulsively now. While it may seem that sharing feelings with others hinders progress, it garners us support that overcomes the isolation of not accepting advice and assistance.

November 3, Solar Eclipse in Scorpio: Baby Steps
Expect power struggles controlling Saturn's conjunction to this New Moon Eclipse. It's not easy to trust people—and sometimes it's just as difficult to trust ourselves. This eclipse, however, is about backing away from pressure, reducing

intensity, and seeking peaceful moments in our lives. Recognizing the gifts that we're given every day can alleviate a profound feeling of hunger, perhaps even despair, through small moments of joy and pleasure.

THE BOTTOM LINE:
YELL FIRE!

The Mayan calendar may have turned over near the end of 2012, but the human story on this planet is far from complete. Nevertheless, we are still in the midst of a period of powerful change that began with the opposition of structural Saturn and explosive Uranus in late 2008, when we experienced the first wave of the worst financial crisis since the Great Depression, along with the subsequent election of Barack Obama. The year 2012 brought the first of seven tense squares between Uranus and transformational Pluto that will recur through 2015, shaking the very foundations of societies around the world. The volatile Uranus-Pluto square is exact on May 20 and November 1, April 21 and December 15, 2014, and March 16, 2015. The long-lasting connection between revolutionary Uranus and volcanic Pluto is already fomenting change on a grand scale, and this will continue for years to come.

It is tempting, though, to gaze back and seek to re-create the relative safety of the past. Joyful Jupiter's entry into cautious and conservative Cancer will bring waves of nostalgia for the "good old days," along with protectionist calls for stronger national borders. Yet the idea that we can return to the past is not a feasible one. The technological cats are out of the bag, and addressing environmental issues alone requires forward, not backward, thinking. Our challenge is to construct new realities based on bold visions and idealistic dreams of a world that does not yet exist. This takes courage in the face of confusion and confidence in the midst of chaos. It's tempting to call out to higher powers to rescue us from the consequences of our actions: suffering evokes cries for help. And yet we are capable of healing ourselves if we finally embrace the twenty-first century instead of retreating to mythical moments of an idealized past.

Inventive Uranus in pioneering Aries is opening new neural pathways that are reshaping our view of reality. Yes, we may encounter moments when thoughts are so strange that we may fear ourselves to be mad. But curious minds, flexible egos, and adaptable emotions allow us to glimpse a more enlightened, evolved, and competent humanity without breaking down. We are challenged to dance with the stranger who enters our heads with perceptions that don't readily fit into our existing intellectual framework. We must find new ways out of the dilemmas that we've created for ourselves. Embracing small discoveries and appreciating surprises are good training techniques: they prepare us to step up to the next level of human evolution and continue the remarkable journey of love and light on planet Earth.

Remember that all of these astrological events are part of the general cosmic weather of the year, but will affect us each differently based upon our individual astrological signs.

SAGITTARIUS
AUGUST–DECEMBER
2012 OVERVIEW

BIG PICTURE SHOW

The freethinking Aquarius Full Moon on **August 1** lights up your 3rd House of Communication to kick off this busy month. A happy trine to beneficent Jupiter in your 7th House of Others brings good news from a friend or colleague. Look beyond your daily routine and make exciting plans for the future as the radiant Leo Sun moves through your 9th House of Adventure until **August 22**. But with Mercury moving backward until **August 8**, it's imperative that you tie up loose ends in existing projects before jumping into what's next. Your belief systems are undergoing a metamorphosis that impacts the way you express yourself. These issues began to surface when transformational Pluto first squared irrepressible Uranus on **June 24**. They're now moving closer together again— their second square is on **September 19**—and magnetic Venus forms stressful aspects to this dynamic duo on **August 15–16**, attracting jealous or controlling people who might try to squelch your desire for independence.

The demonstrative Leo New Moon on **August 17** activates your expansive 9th House, widening your horizons and inspiring you to take bold action to put your big ideas into motion. But just-do-it Mars sneaks into cryptic Scorpio and your 12th House of Secrets on **August 23**, suggesting that you keep your strategy to yourself. Avoid the spotlight while preparing for your next big move, when Mars enters your sign on **October 6**. A second Full Moon this month on **August 31**—this one in dreamy Pisces and your 4th House of Security—draws your attention away from the outer world, invites you to spend more time at home, and revitalizes relationships with your family.

WEDNESDAY 1 ★ ○ Stick to the facts and choose your words carefully

---

THURSDAY 2 ★

FRIDAY 3 ★

SATURDAY 4 ★

SUNDAY 5

MONDAY 6

TUESDAY 7

WEDNESDAY 8

THURSDAY 9

FRIDAY 10

SATURDAY 11

SUNDAY 12

MONDAY 13

TUESDAY 14 ★ **SUPER NOVA DAYS** You receive mixed messages from friends

---

WEDNESDAY 15 ★

THURSDAY 16 ★

FRIDAY 17 ★ ●

SATURDAY 18

SUNDAY 19

MONDAY 20 ★ Avoid the distractions of idle fantasies

TUESDAY 21 ★

WEDNESDAY 22 ★

THURSDAY 23 ★

FRIDAY 24 ★

SATURDAY 25

SUNDAY 26

MONDAY 27

TUESDAY 28

WEDNESDAY 29 ★ Be quiet and listen to your inner voice

THURSDAY 30 ★

FRIDAY 31 ★ ○

★ designates key date

NO EASY ESCAPE

Your career takes center stage this month with Mercury and the Sun spotlighting your 10th House of Public Life until **September 16** and **September 22**, respectively. But action-hero Mars in shrewd Scorpio and your 12th House of Privacy until **October 6** has you working behind the scenes. Fortunately, your concentrated effort goes a long way on **September 3–6**, when Mars forms helpful aspects with impressive Pluto, communicative Mercury, and effusive Jupiter. You receive another boost of energy as popular Venus enters fellow fire sign Leo and your expansive 9th House on **September 6**. However, you could promise more than you're able to deliver or underestimate the complexity of a job when the Sun and Mercury square Jupiter on **September 7–8**. The discerning Virgo New Moon on **September 15** activates your ambitious 10th House and is an excellent time to prioritize your tasks. Focus on one specific goal and set aside other, less important aspirations.

Meanwhile, deeper rumblings are shaking your life as radical Uranus in your 5th House of Self-Expression forms the second of seven life-changing squares to relentless Pluto in your 2nd House of Self-Esteem. Although this aspect is exact on **September 19**—the first was on **June 24**, and the series completes on **March 16, 2015**—you could feel the effects more strongly when it's stressed by mischievous Mercury on the **20th**, Mars and Venus on the **25th–26th**, and the impetuous Aries Full Moon on the **29th**. Your patience wears thin as financial pressures and your desire for personal freedom make you aware of the gulf between what you have and what you want.

SATURDAY 1

SUNDAY 2

MONDAY 3 ★ Watch your temper while making your case

TUESDAY 4 ★

WEDNESDAY 5 ★

THURSDAY 6

FRIDAY 7 ★ You can reach your goals if you practice self-discipline

SATURDAY 8 ★

SUNDAY 9 ★

MONDAY 10 ★

TUESDAY 11

WEDNESDAY 12

THURSDAY 13 ★ Let everyone know what you want

FRIDAY 14 ★

SATURDAY 15 ★ ●

SUNDAY 16 ★

MONDAY 17

TUESDAY 18

WEDNESDAY 19

THURSDAY 20 ★ Seek more balance in your life

FRIDAY 21 ★

SATURDAY 22 ★

SUNDAY 23

MONDAY 24

TUESDAY 25 ★ **SUPER NOVA DAYS** Avoid reckless behavior

WEDNESDAY 26 ★

THURSDAY 27 ★

FRIDAY 28 ★

SATURDAY 29 ★ ○

SUNDAY 30

IN THE ZONE

It looks like you're on a roll this month as Mars jumps into extroverted Sagittarius and your 1st House of Personality on **October 6**, motivating you to assert yourself as you push ahead on all fronts. Your physical vitality is strong, yet you could be so enthusiastic about showing others what you can do that you become overbearing. Fortunately, the socially astute Libra Sun in your 11th House of Friends and Associates sensitizes you to others and helps you balance your aggressive approach until **October 22**. Meanwhile, just prior to the loud arrival of rambunctious Mars in your sign, cerebral Mercury and solemn Saturn enter your 12th House of Spirituality on **October 5** in an ironic move that turns your thoughts inward just as your behavior becomes more highly animated. Although Mercury only stays in mysterious Scorpio until **October 29**, slow-moving Saturn remains in your 12th House of Endings until **December 23, 2014**. This is a long-lasting transit that will require you to retreat from the outer world, redefine your life path, and clear out old emotional baggage. However, it makes sense to get started on these ambitious goals when Saturn harmonizes with visionary Neptune on **October 10** because common sense helps you to ground your dreams.

Powerful waves of expansion and contraction wash over you now as cheerful Jupiter aspects somber Saturn—yet the gracious Libra New Moon on **October 15** falls in your 11th House of Dreams and Wishes, encouraging moderation. The materialistic Taurus Full Moon on **October 29** illuminates your 6th House of Work while thoughtful Mercury enters fun-loving Sagittarius, reminding you that maintaining your daily routine is crucial to keep your life in order and reach your goals.

MONDAY 1

TUESDAY 2

WEDNESDAY 3 ★ The spotlight of recognition shines brightly on you

THURSDAY 4 ★

FRIDAY 5 ★

SATURDAY 6

SUNDAY 7

MONDAY 8

TUESDAY 9 ★ Your intuition won't lead you astray now

WEDNESDAY 10 ★

THURSDAY 11

FRIDAY 12

SATURDAY 13

SUNDAY 14

MONDAY 15 ★ ● SUPER NOVA DAYS You're all fired up

TUESDAY 16 ★

WEDNESDAY 17

THURSDAY 18

FRIDAY 19

SATURDAY 20

SUNDAY 21

MONDAY 22

TUESDAY 23

WEDNESDAY 24

THURSDAY 25 ★ Confront the truth

FRIDAY 26

SATURDAY 27

SUNDAY 28 ★ You could exhaust yourself if you don't pay attention

MONDAY 29 ★ ○

TUESDAY 30

WEDNESDAY 31

GOOD THINGS COME TO THOSE WHO WAIT

This month begins with a bit of excitement as delicious Venus opposes wild Uranus in your 5th House of Love and Creativity on **November 1**. Your vitality is high and your patience is low with impulsive Mars in extroverted Sagittarius until **November 16**. Additionally, you can be hyperactive with inquisitive Mercury also in your sign. But it becomes harder to say what you mean without being misunderstood when the Winged Messenger turns retrograde on **November 6** and backs into enigmatic Scorpio and your 12th House of Secrets on **November 14**. Although Mercury turns direct on **November 26**, releasing you from the past, your thoughts won't be flying free again until it reenters Sagittarius on **December 10**.

You long for emotional connection—or perhaps to eliminate something or someone that's dragging you down—when the profound Scorpio New Moon Solar Eclipse on **November 13** falls in your 12th House of Destiny. But watch out, because moving too quickly is as bad as doing nothing at all on **November 15** when erratic Uranus forms a quirky quincunx with stable Saturn. Mars's shift into sure-footed Capricorn on the **16th** may slow your progress, but improves your chances for success by encouraging sound methods over rash action. Your popularity increases when the bright Sun enters your 1st House of Personality on **November 21**, giving you extra energy. However, vulnerable Venus slips into your reclusive 12th House, tempting you with the idea of solitude. The multifaceted Gemini Full Moon Eclipse on **November 28** joins jubilant Jupiter in your 7th House of Others, confirming that your waiting period is over and that it's time to move ahead in a relationship.

THURSDAY 1 ★ Obligations require you to work more than you wish

---

FRIDAY 2 ★

SATURDAY 3 ★

SUNDAY 4 ★

MONDAY 5

TUESDAY 6 ★ Your optimism about a current relationship is contagious

---

WEDNESDAY 7 ★

THURSDAY 8 ★

FRIDAY 9 ★

SATURDAY 10

SUNDAY 11

MONDAY 12

TUESDAY 13 ★ ● Feed your soul and not just your need for adventure

---

WEDNESDAY 14 ★

THURSDAY 15 ★

FRIDAY 16

SATURDAY 17

SUNDAY 18

MONDAY 19

TUESDAY 20

WEDNESDAY 21

THURSDAY 22

FRIDAY 23 ★ A bit of patience pays off

SATURDAY 24 ★

SUNDAY 25

MONDAY 26

TUESDAY 27 ★ **SUPER NOVA DAYS** Transform fear into love

WEDNESDAY 28 ★ ○

THURSDAY 29 ★

FRIDAY 30

HOME FOR THE HOLIDAYS

This month is all about relationships, because your ruling planet, Jupiter—retrograding in your 7th House of Companions—forms ten separate aspects. Despite the significant role that others play in your life now, it's up to you to take the lead as the radiant Sun moves through your sign, illuminating your 1st House of Self until **December 21**. Your mental acuity helps you to communicate what's important as long as you don't fall prey to exaggerations when gregarious Mercury visits risk-taking Sagittarius on **December 10–31**. You thoroughly enjoy being you—a wonderful state of affairs for the holiday season—while pleasure-seeking Venus visits your adventurous sign, from **December 15** until **January 8, 2013**. However, there are others to consider, too, and the tension becomes palpable as your desire for independence and exploration pulls one way while enticing opportunities and good fellowship pull the other. This is most noticeable when oppositions to jolly Jupiter are formed by the Sun on **December 2**, Mercury on **December 17**, and Venus on **December 22**. It's wise to address unstable dynamics between you and your spouse, friend, or colleague when cosmic heavyweights Pluto and Saturn move into the picture on **December 20–22**, forming uneasy quincunxes with overextending Jupiter.

The cavalier Sagittarius New Moon on **December 13** could make you feel invincible, as if nothing can stop you from reaching your goals. Although positive thought can propel you far, this lunation's disquieting semisquare to prudent Saturn helps you acknowledge that time and resources are limited. If you're overextended, the nurturing Cancer Full Moon on the **28th** illuminates your 8th House of Regeneration, reflecting your need to revitalize your spirit by spending holiday time with friends and family.

SATURDAY 1 ★ You're restless without knowing why

SUNDAY 2 ★

MONDAY 3

TUESDAY 4

WEDNESDAY 5

THURSDAY 6

FRIDAY 7

SATURDAY 8

SUNDAY 9

MONDAY 10 ★ **SUPER NOVA DAYS** Put your enthusiasm and joy into words

---

TUESDAY 11 ★

WEDNESDAY 12 ★

THURSDAY 13 ★ ●

FRIDAY 14 ★

SATURDAY 15

SUNDAY 16

MONDAY 17

TUESDAY 18

WEDNESDAY 19

THURSDAY 20

FRIDAY 21

SATURDAY 22

SUNDAY 23

MONDAY 24

TUESDAY 25 ★ Place your long-term goals into proper perspective

---

WEDNESDAY 26 ★

THURSDAY 27

FRIDAY 28 ★ ○ Make a bold statement of your individuality

SATURDAY 29 ★

SUNDAY 30 ★

MONDAY 31 ★

2013 HOROSCOPE

SAGITTARIUS

NOVEMBER 22–DECEMBER 21

SAGITTARIUS 2013 OVERVIEW

You'll enjoy many great opportunities to go public with your plans and make personal and professional connections this year. Your optimistic ruling planet, Jupiter, is in versatile Gemini and your 7th House of Partners until June 25, empowering you to enhance your image, launch new projects, and seek out advantageous business contacts. **Your willingness to adapt to a wide variety of situations opens doors that are closed to less flexible individuals.** However, it's tempting to accept others too quickly when hopeful Jupiter in sometimes superficial Gemini inhibits you from seeing past the surface to recognize their subtle strengths and weaknesses. People may find you attractive for less-than-substantial reasons, as well, reminding you that confidence easily gained can be lost just as readily. While clever ideas and instant chemistry can point the way to meaningful alliances, a deeper analysis of your needs and others' assets is a key to turning these potentially beneficial unions into reality.

It's time to take your relationships to the next

level or break them up on the rocks of failure on June 25, when Jupiter enters nurturing Cancer and your 8th House of Intimacy. This yearlong transit opens emotional channels that are comforting when you trust the one you're with, but can feel suffocating when your partner is too needy and insecure. Nevertheless, if you don't allow abstractions and big ideas to drown out your emotional instincts, the benefits you receive from your relationships may be greater than ever. **Exploring feelings that you might not be able to explain can make the difference between your fulfillment and endless frustration.** Saturn, the planet of hard, cold reality, is in watery Scorpio, where it's trawling for buried desires and doubts in your 12th House of Soul Consciousness. This demanding planet is telling you to look into your dark closet of fear. Facing your limits directly can release their grip on your psyche, which has kept you from reaching your full potential.

Swimming through the mysteries of emotion is not your favorite exercise, but you might be pleasantly surprised by what you discover now. On July 17, visionary Jupiter forms harmonious aspects with practical Saturn and imaginative

Neptune. This Grand Water Trine marks a magical moment when you can reach a perfect balance between the ideal and the real, placing you on track to finding more inspiration in your public life. **Success is more likely if you contribute to organizations that serve others or pursue a career aligned with your highest hopes.** The Jupiter-Saturn trine repeats on December 12, but you may not reach the top of the mountain until the final occurrence on May 24, 2014. Nevertheless, your good judgment and strong strategic sense are pointing you in the right direction. There's no need to advertise your plans prematurely as the life-changing alchemy of this Grand Water Trine is better nourished by your own inner voice than by the input of others. Trusting your instincts is essential, even if they betray you at times, because learning to listen to yourself is the most valuable lesson of the year.

PLAYING THE FIELD

Relationships rock with boisterous Jupiter starting the year in your 7th House of Partners and finishing it in your 8th House of Deep Sharing. It's hard to avoid flirtations even if you're already in a committed partnership. Promises can be made without conviction with irreverent Uranus in your 5th House of Romance, stirring restless feelings and increasing your taste for extreme experiences and radical risk taking. You grow more cautious with Jupiter's shift into protective Cancer and your intimate 8th House on June 25. However, the Sun's smooth trines to realistic Saturn and dreamy Neptune on June 26 draw you out of your shell and enable you to successfully pursue a fantasy that might elude you at other times. The impulsive Aries Full Moon Eclipse on October 18 can pull the rug out from under a love affair. Your partner may suddenly not be available, or your own boredom might put an end to a playful but short-lived adventure. Knowing the difference between a fast fling and a lasting thing brings gain instead of pain.

CUT TO THE CHASE

Be discriminating about where you invest your time, money, and energy this year. Opportunities to change jobs, reach new customers, or make a public splash tempt you to scatter your resources. The pragmatic Virgo Full Moon shines in your 10th House of Career on February 25, exposing problems if you're spread too thin. If offers come your way, narrow your options and pick only the best of the litter. Working with more conservative colleagues who are reliable—even if they're less than passionate—provides a healthy balance to your natural enthusiasm. On September 5, the efficient Virgo New Moon in your professional 10th House is favorably aligned with Jupiter, which allows you to recognize how perfecting your skills in one specific area is more lucrative than trying to be a Jack (or Jane) of all trades.

WHEELER-DEALER

You gain a fresh perspective on finances with the ambitious Capricorn New Moon in your 2nd House of Resources on January 11. Valuable Venus's conjunction with Pluto and square to innovative Uranus during this lunation can open your eyes to unconventional ways to increase your income. Learning the art of the deal, when to gamble, or how to get the most money for your work is an ongoing story with profitable Pluto in your 2nd House of Self-Worth. You should seek good economic advice and, perhaps, forge a business partnership after opportunistic Jupiter enters your 8th House of Shared Resources on June 25. Leveraging your relationships by recognizing the needs of others and making connections among people who can help one another will earn you more than you'd get operating independently or working for an hourly wage. Just be cautious and double-check every detail when trickster Mercury is retrograde in your 8th House on June 26–July 20.

RUN YOUR OWN RACE

Speedy Mars enters steady Taurus and your 6th House of Health on April 20, helping you settle into a regular routine of physical activity that won't wear you out. Avoid excessive workouts or burning the candle at both ends, especially with a pair of eclipses in May. A Solar Eclipse in Taurus on May 9 joins Mars in your 6th House, tempting you to push too hard. The Sagittarius Full Moon Eclipse on May 25 is square to squishy Neptune; this tense aspect with the planet of dissolution represents a lack of boundaries or self-control that can lead to fatigue and vulnerability. Staying within your limits instead of trying to keep up with others is key to your physical well-being this year.

OUT WITH THE OLD

You continue to focus this year on acting with sensitivity to both your own needs and the needs of those with whom you live with compassionate Neptune in your 4th House of Home and Family. You may pick up mixed signals as Mercury's retrograde in your 4th House on February 23–March 17 dredges up old emotional issues while the psychic Pisces New Moon on March 11 prompts fresh ideas and spiritual interests. Artistic Venus and passionate Mars join with this lunation, inspiring more love and beauty in your household. However, it's best to clean up unfinished business before you start redecorating the place or invite someone to move in with you.

DUTY-FREE ZONE

Your hunger for travel and learning continues unabated this year, but don't let someone talk you into taking a trip when the bold Leo Full Moon illuminates your 9th House of Faraway Places on January 26. Spontaneous Uranus's trine to the Moon can spur an exciting opportunity, yet a lunar square with constraining Saturn indicates delays, difficulties, or costs that exceed your expectations. A better time to hit the road arrives on August 6, when thrill-seeking Uranus zaps the gallant Leo New Moon unencumbered by the restrictions of heavy-duty Saturn.

BURIED TREASURE

Your spiritual journeys take you down complex paths, because Saturn in emotionally intense Scorpio occupies your 12th House of Divinity all year. Facing fears can be a painful but productive way to remove obstacles from your life. The Scorpio New Moon Eclipse on November 3 could drive you to the depths of your soul, but a supportive sextile from Mars in skillful Virgo will show you the methods you can use to rebuild your faith from the ground up.

RICK & JEFF'S TIP FOR THE YEAR
Follow Your Instincts

Your most important challenge this year is making the best choices in relationships. Many people may find you desirable, providing additional chances to socialize personally and professionally. Yet good might not be good enough if it keeps you from connecting with the person who can offer you so much more. Slow down and take the time to listen to what's in your heart instead of allowing impulsive thinking to dictate your decisions.

JANUARY

UPHILL CLIMB

You're naturally a person of big ideas and adventurous experiences who is typically more into doing things than having things. But material concerns may weigh heavily on your mind this month with five planets passing through goal-oriented Capricorn and your 2nd House of Income. January begins with the willful Sun, brainy Mercury, and obsessive Pluto in this economically oriented part of your chart. Resourceful Venus joins them on **January 8** to reward your persistence, patience, and careful execution of a plan. On **January 11**, the orderly Capricorn New Moon supplies practical energy that you can apply with a clear sense of purpose. If you can shift from a strategic big-picture view to a perspective from down in the trenches where you're able to efficiently take care of business, you will overcome almost any obstacle. But if you're stuck in a dead-end job without an exciting vision of your future, spending time and money to learn the tools of another trade can turn your career in a desirable new direction.

It's time to take a break from your hard work

when Mercury and the Sun fly into unconventional Aquarius and your 3rd House of Communication on **January 19**. New connections and original ideas bring more variety and excitement to your daily life. Interesting individuals are more likely to cross your path and inspire you with sparkling conversations. The travel bug may bite with the outgoing Leo Full Moon in your 9th House of Faraway Places on the **26th**, but Saturn's restrictive square might delay your takeoff. However, your ruling planet Jupiter's forward turn on the **30th** in your 7th House of Relationships attracts helpful allies and raises your public profile.

KEEP IN MIND THIS MONTH

Establishing a steady pace of productivity and sticking to it may lack the excitement you crave, but the tangible results this produces are worth the sacrifice.

KEY DATES

★ **JANUARY 4–5**
shifting into overdrive
A high-octane trine between hyperactive
Mars and exuberant Jupiter gets you moving
physically and mentally on **January 4**. Your
over-the-top enthusiasm, though, may
motivate you to oversell or overreach. A tight-
fisted Venus-Saturn semisquare is a reminder
that limited resources or lack of support from
others may constrain your efforts. Still, it's
nearly impossible to narrow your focus as
mental Mercury misaligns with a quincunx
to Jupiter on the **5th**. You might try to skirt
reality with flippant statements that are
unlikely to accurately assess your situation.
While stretching your mind reveals untapped
potential, it's wise to do some serious
research before you make any promises.

★ **JANUARY 11**
unnecessary distractions
Your attention is scattered in several different
directions when the commitment of today's

earthy Capricorn New Moon is diffused by an awkward sesquisquare between the creative Sun and boundless Jupiter in breezy Gemini. While you find it useful to consider alternative paths to your goals, choose one and stick to it. If you find yourself entangled in exhausting explanations to people who don't understand what you're doing, it might be best to save your breath unless they're critical to your plan.

★ **JANUARY 14**
separation of work and play
Good intentions aren't enough today when friendly Mercury and lovable Venus form difficult aspects with promising Jupiter. Minor matters can take on a larger-than-life importance that's out of proportion with your needs. Trying to charm someone (or being charmed by them) is more about entertainment and flattery than getting work done. Keep the value of your time, energy, and resources firmly in mind to avoid spending too much on discussions that lead nowhere. Having fun is fine as long as it doesn't get in the way of your higher priorities.

★ **JANUARY 22**
lucky charms
You can think and speak with considerable
skill today, actively contributing to brilliant
conversations. Quicksilver Mercury's favorable
aspects to inventive Uranus and philosophical
Jupiter make you an energetic and effective
spokesperson for your beliefs. Your positive
perspective could receive an additional boost if
long-awaited news finally comes through.

SUPER NOVA DAYS

★ **JANUARY 25–26**
delusions of grandeur
Your powers of persuasion are strong with an
inspirational Sun-Jupiter trine on **January 25**.
However, have your facts in order since a
demanding Mercury-Saturn square will
reveal any flaws in your argument. The **26th** is
complicated by the contrast between a playful
Venus-Jupiter sesquisquare and a take-no-
prisoners Mars-Pluto semisquare. Don't let
your unrealistic expectations set you up for
disappointment—delight can be yours if you
more carefully measure your desire.

FEBRUARY

LEARN FROM YOUR PAST

Domestic matters take precedence this month with a parade of planets floating through your 4th House of Home and Family. On **February 1**, energetic Mars swims into sensitive Pisces and this part of your chart to stir up the emotional waters in your household. Long-lingering issues may surface to provoke conflict, yet this transit can also provide you the drive to turn your living space into a launching pad for long-term ambitions. Sweet Venus's entry into airy Aquarius on the **1st** provides a dash of objectivity and spurs collaboration in conversations with creative people. Communicative Mercury moves into mystical Pisces on **February 5**, enhancing your psychic powers. However, your hypersensitivity also gives you an extra layer of vulnerability. Mercury's retrograde turn in your introspective 4th House on the **23rd** brings up issues from the past to inspire your imagination or confuse you with uncertainty.

You're blessed with original thinking on **February 10**—a gift of the conceptual Aquarius New Moon in your 3rd House of Information.

However, your unconventional visions of the future might not be comfortable for others as a Venus-Saturn square on the **11th** evokes resistance from conservative individuals. The Sun's passage into Pisces on the **18th** supplies courage and compassion when you must deal with complicated emotions, but forgiveness is your key to applying them effectively. Obligations at work can reach a critical point on the **25th** when the perfectionist Virgo Full Moon lights up your 10th House of Career. A lunar square to limitless Jupiter in jittery Gemini could overwhelm you with a million and one tiny tasks. Fortunately, the Moon's perceptive trine with purging Pluto requires you to eliminate unnecessary obligations to clarify your professional priorities.

KEEP IN MIND THIS MONTH

The key to the happiness you seek is a sense of security. You can create this by attending to personal issues and working toward a more nurturing environment at home.

KEY DATES

★ FEBRUARY 4
chasing unicorns

You might feel like you're spinning in circles without getting much done as action-planet Mars joins mysterious Neptune. Pursuing illusions or playing the martyr is exhausting, so rein yourself in before you run out of gas. Still, this sensitive transit also helps you make a little magic at home by engaging in creative activities and showing tenderness to those you love.

SUPER NOVA DAYS

★ FEBRUARY 6–10
fasten your seat belt

You enjoy new forms of pleasure on the **6th** with an adventurous Venus-Uranus sextile. An intuitive Mercury-Neptune conjunction helps you read between the lines, yet you risk being sloppy with facts or falling for someone's misleading story. A Venus-Jupiter trine on the **7th** amplifies your social charms, attracts generous people, and brightens your day. This delightful mood may be shaken with a verbally aggressive Mercury-Mars conjunction on **February 8**. While this planetary pair can sharpen thinking and empower words, you might go to extremes when eloquent Mercury squares opinionated Jupiter on the **9th** and excitable Mars makes the same aspect on the **10th**. The Aquarius New Moon contributes to these patterns by urging you to promote your ideas and act with enthusiasm. Managing these energetic wild horses effectively can enable you to be very productive, but letting them run freely could trigger conflicts.

★ **FEBRUARY 15–16**
efficiency expert
You get a grip on your passion and apply it very effectively thanks to two favorable connections of dynamic Mars. A supportive sextile with surgical Pluto on **February 15** cuts through clutter and connects you with the core of an issue. A responsible Mars-Saturn on the **16th** is equally focused and highly productive. Anger can be converted into positive action and problems solved by behaving with patience and maturity.

★ **FEBRUARY 21**
sentimental journey
You may be wistful about the past as the Sun
joins Neptune in your 4th House of Roots.
Idealizing your childhood or someone close
to you lifts your spirits and inspires new
aspirations even though this also can be an
easy way to escape the reality of the here and
now. Take some time off from your obligations
to bask in the light of possibilities that, for the
moment, might seem out of reach.

★ **FEBRUARY 25–26**
stick to the point
You incline toward excess and overstating your
beliefs at the best of times, Sagittarius—a
tendency that's stoked on **February 25** by
an overblown Sun-Jupiter square. However,
even if you're off somewhere on cloud nine, a
sharp-eyed Mercury-Mars conjunction on the
26th motivates you to turn clever ideas into
constructive action. Don't waste time getting
caught up in petty arguments; they distract
you from the real tasks at hand.

MARCH

HOME IS WHERE THE HEART IS

The fires of passion and creativity burn brightly in you this month. You can set the stage for the excitement by beautifying your residence or resolving family squabbles with the compassionate Pisces New Moon on **March 11**. This lunation in your 4th House of Roots conjuncts gracious Venus, inviting harmony into your home, healing old wounds, nourishing faith in yourself, and stimulating your imagination. It won't take you long to put your dreams into action, because irrepressible Mars rams into impatient Aries and your 5th House of Romance on the **12th**, provoking impulsive and sometimes reckless behavior. However, it's better to carefully test the waters than immediately plunge into a love affair or make a sudden business move. Logical Mercury's forward turn in your foundational 4th House on **March 17** gives you the information and healthy perspective you need to guide your actions more skillfully.

On **March 20** the Sun enters ardent Aries, marking the Spring Equinox, and adds fuel to your 5th House of Self-Expression. Amorous

Venus follows the next day, further enhancing your ability to attract attention, entertain others, and display your creative gifts. Your desire for immediate satisfaction can provoke foolhardy actions in matters of the heart. This is a terrific time to enjoy yourself by reigniting the flame of love to revive a fading relationship or to pursue a new one. Just be careful about assuming that one night of bliss guarantees a lifetime of happiness. Downsizing your expectations ensures that the pleasure you receive won't be too costly. The partnership-oriented Libra Full Moon on the **27th** shines in your 11th House of Community, balancing your desire for pleasure with a willingness to honor what others need.

KEEP IN MIND THIS MONTH

Making yourself more comfortable at home doesn't mean that you're lazy; instead, it gives you the confidence you need to be even more expressive and outgoing than ever.

KEY DATES

★ **MARCH 4**
less is more
Today you risk seeing people, experiences, and objects as more valuable than they are thanks to evaluative Venus's stressful square with excessive Jupiter. You may also be so optimistic that you overindulge in pleasurable activities. While it's good to stretch your social boundaries and broaden your tastes, be sure you also maintain your moral compass.

★ **MARCH 7–9**
step by step
You're thinking solidly on **March 7**, when cerebral Mercury's favorable aspects with Saturn and Pluto deepen your perceptions, but you may not get the results you want if an obstreperous Mars-Saturn sesquisquare slows your progress. Incremental gains won't satisfy your need for speed, but they will eventually take you where you want to go. You may throw patience out the window on the **9th** when a verbose Mercury-Jupiter square

overloads you with information and weakens your focus. It's tempting to overstate if you're enthusiastic about something, but careless speech could create unrealistic expectations: More modest claims allow you to make your point and maintain credibility.

★ **MARCH 16**
buried treasure
The Sun's sesquisquare with strict Saturn can evoke painful memories. You're not one to live in the past, yet self-doubt or delays caused by others could lead you to question your competence. However, if you step around your emotions, you can find answers in unexpected places. A creative quintile between artful Venus and insightful Pluto garners support from others and reveals unseen assets that could save a wounded relationship or provide you with the resources needed to take care of business.

★ **MARCH 22–23**
lightning strikes
An explosive Mars-Uranus conjunction in your 5th House of Fun and Games brings out

your wild side on **March 22**. Innovation and spontaneity are strong, yet your need for freedom can trigger rebellious behavior. Going too far leads to disapproval as clumsy Jupiter forms an awkward quincunx with cynical Saturn on the **23rd**.

SUPER NOVA DAYS

★ **MARCH 28–31**
crazy love
New pleasures and sudden eruptions of desire put you in strange situations on **March 28**, when sexy Venus, the heartfelt Sun, and reactive Uranus meet in your romantic 5th House. Although you're wise to experiment with your attitude and appearance, you might go to extreme measures with an overbearing Jupiter-Pluto quincunx on the **29th**. Venus's tense square with suspicious Pluto on the **31st** increases your sensitivity to manipulation and may force you to let go of a radical idea. Happily, Venus's favorable sextile with bountiful Jupiter should compensate you with other rewards.

APRIL

HIT THE GROUND RUNNING

You can practically count on finding new forms of fun and experiencing breakthroughs in creativity this month. The pioneering Aries New Moon falls in your 5th House of Self-Expression on **April 10**, offering fresh opportunities to demonstrate your talents and showcase your desirability. This Sun-Moon conjunction is joined by spicy Mars and sultry Venus, stimulating romantic impulses and flirtatious behavior. You're ready to take the lead in your personal life and in any professional situation that calls for putting on a good show. Fleet-footed Mercury blasts into uncontainable Aries and your 5th House of Spontaneity on the **13th**, sparking even more bright ideas and brash statements. The fun quotient in your life is definitely on the upswing, but making it last long enough to produce enduring results could be a major challenge for you. Living in the moment comes easily to your adventurous sign, but when excitement cools you struggle to maintain your interest.

The pace starts to change when sensual Venus enters stable Taurus and your 6th House of Employment on **April 15**. Slowing down to enjoy your work, instead of rushing to get things done, can improve your skills and earn you additional approval for your efforts. The Sun and Mars enter Taurus on the **19th** and **20th**, placing more emphasis on your job and increasing your commitment to excellence. Your persistent efforts at self-improvement are admirable, but a stubborn streak could make you less flexible about changing your methods. The emotional Scorpio Lunar Eclipse on **April 25** rattles your 12th House of Secrets, where it could expose an inconvenient truth. Saturn's conjunction to this Full Moon reminds you to redouble your efforts to work through your fears and self-limitations instead of taking the easy way out and settling for less.

KEEP IN MIND THIS MONTH

Investing more of yourself in the activities that you enjoy ensures that they will continue to be significant sources of pleasure for many years to come.

KEY DATES

★ **APRIL 1**
window of opportunity
You can impress others easily today when
the confident Aries Sun in your 5th House of
Self-Expression forms a supportive sextile
with lucky Jupiter in your 7th House of Others.
It's an excellent time to make a sales pitch or
initiate a professional relationship. Enrolling
people in your plan works especially well if
you can match your enthusiasm with your
command of the facts.

★ **APRIL 6-8**
smoke and mirrors
Your taste for fantasy could provide you
with a magical day on **April 6**, when squishy
semisquares from dreamy Neptune to the
cosmic lovers, Venus and Mars, turn your
imagination's volume up high. Still, you can
roam so far from reality that you may have a
hard time finding your way back. The urge to
connect emotionally and physically intensifies
when Venus joins Mars in your playful 5th

House on the **7th**. It's all too easy to overlook someone's flaws and see him or her through rose-colored glasses. A Sun-Neptune semisquare on the **8th** underscores the likelihood that what you're seeing is not what you'll get.

★ **APRIL 14–15**
blessing in disguise
A careless Venus-Jupiter semisquare on **April 14** lures you into believing a story that's either incomplete or not on the level. If this doesn't concern a serious issue, it could be more bothersome than problematic. However, you can quickly adjust to bad judgment when a brilliant Mercury-Jupiter quintile on the **15th** shows you how to fix mistakes and correct misunderstandings.

SUPER NOVA DAYS
★ **APRIL 20–21**
curb your enthusiasm
The smartest way to use a bright idea is to test it before fully committing to it. An optimistic Sun-Jupiter semisquare and

ingenious Mercury-Uranus conjunction on
April 20 lights up your mind with brainstorms
of originality. But a tendency to act too quickly
or say too much too soon can undermine your
plan before it gets off the ground. You might
feel like you can do anything on the **21st** when
zealous Jupiter stresses superhero Mars.
Fighting for your beliefs may seem like a noble
endeavor, but passion alone doesn't prove that
you're right. When the truth is on your side,
you can present it in a calm, self-confident
manner.

★ **APRIL 28**
no second chances
You have little room for error today thanks
to the Sun's opposition to demanding Saturn.
Take your time with a difficult task and get it
done correctly the first time. If you lack the
skill to handle a particular job, let an expert
show you how it's done.

MAY

GONE WITH THE WIND

Evaluating your contentment, or lack thereof, with personal and professional partners challenges you to step back from your daily distractions to take a longer range view of your relationships this month. The most significant astrological event is the Sagittarius Full Moon Eclipse on **May 25**, which falls in your 1st House of Personality. Every major decision is fraught with uncertainty, which is why adaptability is essential now. You try to lock into a steadier routine at work when the dependable Taurus New Moon on **May 9** activates your 6th House of Habits. Your desires for constancy and security are strong, yet this lunation is a Solar Eclipse that's more about altering patterns than holding on to them. Fortunately, your capacity to skillfully shift gears is supported by a slew of planets entering adaptable Gemini and your 7th House of Others. Sociable Venus starts the parade on **May 9**, followed by verbal Mercury on the **15th**, the willful Sun on the **20th**, and mobile Mars on the **31st**.

Making connections should come easily now, but being discriminating about who you

share your time and energy with is critical.
The long-lasting Uranus-Pluto square that
began on **June 24, 2012**, and repeats on **May 20**
emphasizes your 5th House of Play and can act
like a lightning rod that attracts exciting people
into your life. Fascinating individuals can be like
shiny objects that grab your attention but have
little real value. A career-shaping Jupiter-Saturn
sesquisquare, also on the **20th**, reminds you
to think strategically instead of overreacting to
immediate events.

KEEP IN MIND THIS MONTH

*You must prioritize your long-term goals to avoid those
fleeting temptations that look good in the moment . . .
but don't have the substance to fulfill your dreams.*

KEY DATES

★ **MAY 2**

talk is cheap

You're popping with bright ideas and enjoying lively conversations today while chatty Mercury forms an energetic semisquare with buoyant Jupiter. However, you run the risk of turning one small factoid into a bigger story than is necessary. Making mountains out of molehills isn't productive and could become rather costly. It's great to open your mind to new ideas as long as you don't compromise your ability to critically evaluate them.

★ **MAY 7**

no more drama

A conjunction of argumentative Mercury and combative Mars triggers intense conversations. This contentious union occurs in resistant Taurus and your 6th House of Work and Service, which is likely to add more pressure on the job. Dealing with a stubborn person can be frustrating, especially when you're trying to learn something new or establish a different system. Try to focus on the task at hand instead of getting sidetracked by personal issues; it's a good way to reap the benefits of your shrewd competence without creating unnecessary conflict.

★ **MAY 13–15**
just say no
An escapist Venus-Neptune square on **May 13** blurs your judgment, especially when you're projecting your fantasies onto someone else. This delicious feeling may not be rooted in reality—so enjoy the experience, but don't make any serious commitments. Besides, you may change your mind quickly as Mercury shifts from a tense aspect with jumpy Uranus on the **13th** to one with inscrutable Pluto on the **14th**. Flirtatious Venus in your 7th House of Relationships encounters delays and possible rejection with a quincunx to Saturn on the **15th**. Being choosier about your companions will eliminate individuals who wouldn't be desirable allies.

★ **MAY 24**

cocktail party chit-chat

A sociable Mercury-Venus conjunction is likely to make you more captivating to others, enabling you to attract a charming person. It's easy to find interesting things to talk about as long as you avoid serious subjects. Luckily, you can enjoy some lighthearted play without worrying about long-term expectations.

SUPER NOVA DAYS

★ **MAY 27–28**

sweet as sugar

Mercury's conjunction with magnanimous Jupiter gives impact to your words on **May 27**. You have plenty of information to share without coming across as a know-it-all. Lovely Venus's conjunction with propitious Jupiter on the **28th** continues a positive people trend because you're able to gain appreciation and draw interesting individuals into your life. But be wary of someone who always chatters but never listens. Their compliments are flattering, yet may lack sincerity. Flirting and teasing are sweet, but don't have the staying power.

JUNE

RAISING THE STAKES

It's time to take relationships to the next level—or recognize that it may be best to let some go. June begins with the Sun in friendly Gemini and your 7th House of Partners, which enlivens personal and professional unions. However, complications could start to arise when amenable Venus shifts into sensitive Cancer and your 8th House of Deep Sharing on **June 2**. Financial and emotional rewards may grow, but you might need to compromise your independence and pay more attention to the needs of others. On **June 8**, the inquisitive Gemini New Moon in your 7th House invites entertaining people into your life. Bright ideas are sparked by flames of interest that can burn out as quickly as they begin, so don't make serious commitments without further investigation.

Relationships deepen when the Sun enters Cancer and your 8th House of Transformation on **June 21**, marking the Summer Solstice. Navigating murky emotional waters isn't your favorite activity, yet the vulnerability it can trigger opens hearts and strengthens alliances.

Money matters may come to a head when the responsible Capricorn Full Moon shines in your 2nd House of Resources on **June 23**. Commit yourself to righting your economic ship and patiently cultivate your talents to set yourself on a firmer financial foundation. Saturn's stabilizing sextile to the Full Moon can help you uncover hidden assets and tame your spending habits. Joyful Jupiter's entry into caring Cancer on the **25th** is the beginning of a one-year journey through your 8th House that's likely to bring you the assistance of generous individuals who appreciate your abilities. You'll reconnect with potential supporters when Mercury the Messenger turns retrograde in your 8th House of Deep Sharing on **June 26**.

KEEP IN MIND THIS MONTH

You're usually more comfortable giving than receiving, yet learning how to receive the love and approval of others is a more valuable lesson now.

KEY DATES

★ **JUNE 1**
dancing in the dark
Expect strange encounters when the Sun in your interactive 7th House forms an awkward quincunx with Pluto and a clever sextile with Uranus. The former evokes suspicion, secrecy, and power struggles, but its higher purpose is to purge unrealistic expectations in partnerships and to focus you on the essential work you have to do together. The latter is a free-and-easy aspect that lets bygones be bygones as you open yourself to new and unconventional ways to connect with inventive individuals.

★ **JUNE 7–8**
off the beaten track
Macho Mars in your 7th House of Others attracts impatient individuals into your world. But don't rush into agreements with them on **June 7**, when a stressful square between unstoppable Mars and nebulous Neptune takes you on a wild goose chase

that costs you time, energy, and credibility. Go ahead and enjoy an escape from reality with a playful partner, but beware spreading yourself too thin on the **8th** as the diverse distractions of the flighty Gemini New Moon pull you in several directions at once. Stern Saturn, though, forms a corrective quincunx with impetuous Mars that can impose harsh penalties for careless behavior.

SUPER NOVA DAYS

★ **JUNE 17–19**
learning to fly

You're at your innovative best on **June 17** when you hook up with an open-minded individual to solve sticky problems or initiate creative activities. Mars forms a smart sextile with quirky Uranus in your 5th House of Self-Expression that can combine play and productivity. An instant attraction might be so exciting that you toss caution to the wind. The buoyancy you're feeling increases when the radiant Sun joins cheerful Jupiter in your 7th House of Partners on the **19th**. Your high hopes are probably justified, so go public with an idea, make a professional pitch, or pursue a personal relationship. Just remember that promises come easily—yet turning them into reality requires a concrete plan and consistent follow through.

★ **JUNE 27–28**
no rest for the weary
You're dreaming of faraway places and distant lovers on **June 27**, when vivacious Venus strides into dramatic Leo and your 9th House of Travel. Paying attention to immediate obligations takes priority on the **28th** as reckless Mars is slowed by a stressful sesquisquare from authoritative Saturn. You may be held accountable for tasks that you've either ignored or not completed well enough. Don't let resentment waste your time and keep you from buckling down to meet your responsibilities.

JULY

THE JOURNEY WITHIN

This is a very significant month—but it's more about what's going on inside you than external events. On **July 17**, your philosophical ruling planet, Jupiter, forms a Grand Water Trine with serious Saturn and spiritual Neptune. This uncommon pattern touches the depths of your soul to provide insights into the most intimate areas of your life. Jupiter in your 8th House of Deep Sharing illuminates the heart of relationships and connects that awareness with your 12th House of Secrets and your 4th House of Home and Family. You may not be able to put what you're learning into words, but a profound sense of inner knowing can guide you to make wise decisions about your long-term goals. The moody Cancer New Moon in your 8th House on **July 8** squares surprising Uranus, spurring a sudden shift of feelings or circumstances in close emotional and professional partnerships. You must be more sensitive on the **13th**, when proactive Mars shifts into protective Cancer, if you hope to keep alliances on track.

You slowly begin to think more about collaborating with others with rational Mercury's forward turn in your 8th House on **July 20**, but the unconventional Aquarius Full Moon on the **22nd** is loaded with mixed messages. This lunation in your 3rd House of Information encourages you to be receptive to fresh ideas and new channels of communication. However, its square to restrictive Saturn provokes resistance that may complicate exchanges of information. Delays and inner doubts demand that you study the situation carefully and organize your thoughts before expressing them openly. Yet the Sun's entry into theatrical Leo and your 9th House of Big Ideas later in the day tempts you to jump the gun, which should be avoided at all costs.

KEEP IN MIND THIS MONTH

Tuning in with your feelings may not produce immediate answers, but they will provide more valuable insights than counting on your rational mind alone.

KEY DATES

★ **JULY 1–4**
look but don't leap

It's easy to be grumpy on **July 1** with an opposition from possessive Pluto darkening the Sun with control issues while ominous Saturn inhibits pleasure with a square to needy Venus. Patiently weigh the costs and benefits of any partnership, and you'll make more responsible decisions. An electrifying Sun-Uranus square on the **4th**, though, provokes spontaneous reactions or attracts unreliable people. You may be tempted to radically alter the course of a relationship, but it's smarter to wait until things settle down before making your move.

★ **JULY 9**
listen up!

Retrograde Mercury backs over the Sun in your 8th House of Intimacy and Transformation, providing a second chance to discuss delicate partnership issues. Although you may have very strong feelings, it's helpful to listen carefully to others instead of simply pushing your point of view. A real exchange can be difficult when intense emotions are involved, but avoid dramatic language if your intention is to resolve issues without inciting a meltdown.

★ **JULY 13**
the high cost of love
You may play too hard, pay too much, or expect more from someone than he or she can deliver today when pleasure-seeking Venus in your 9th House of Adventure forms an overamped semisquare with indulgent Jupiter that can mar your judgment. Although you love to stretch your boundaries in search of big experiences, use a bit of self-restraint to avoid spending more love, money, or goodwill than you can afford.

SUPER NOVA DAYS

★ **JULY 19–22**
soft launch
Your dreams seem more real than ever when concrete Saturn trines illusory Neptune on **July 19**. The next day, dynamic Mars forms

an emotional Grand Water Trine with Saturn and Neptune, motivating you to take decisive action. The enthusiastic Mars-Jupiter conjunction on **July 22** in defensive Cancer and your 8th House of Intimacy suggests that gaining the cooperation of a key partner could be challenging, but gently expressing your feelings should lead to success. The Sun enters brassy Leo and Venus slips into demure Virgo on the same day, mixing enthusiasm with caution. Starting a new project or planning a fabulous vacation with a loved one requires a mutual understanding if it's going to work.

★ **JULY 27-28**
labor of love
You'll need hard work and dedication on **July 27** as a Mars-Pluto opposition and a Sun-Saturn square seem to offer limited return for maximum effort. If you can slow down to focus on a tough task or deal with a difficult-to-please person, though, you could see a sweet outcome when resourceful Venus forms a supportive sextile with benevolent Jupiter on the **28th**.

AUGUST

SEEDS OF CHANGE

The deep rumbling you may be feeling now is the beginning of a process that could radically alter your life by next spring. Visionary Jupiter in your 8th House of Deep Sharing makes the first in a series of three oppositions with transformational Pluto on **August 7** and the first of three squares with revolutionary Uranus on **August 21**. Pluto can provoke a power struggle or financial squeeze, while Uranus incites a desire to get away from it all. On the positive side, the intensity of these aspects motivates you to maximize your abilities and seek new sources of inspiration through creative activities with children or, perhaps, an unconventional love affair. The impact of these urges climaxes on **April 20, 2014**, when these transits are complete. The Leo New Moon on **August 6** falls in your 9th House of Higher Truth, opening your mind to a new direction in life with its harmonious trine to progressive Uranus. Temper an impulse to act too quickly; unexpected moves may not be well received by others, who need more time to understand your change of plans.

Intellectual Mercury's shift into proud Leo and your educational 9th House increases your thirst for learning and ramps up your powers of persuasion on **August 8**. Cooperative Venus moves into gracious Libra and your 11th House of Social Networking on the **16th** to stimulate your interest in community service and attract new friends. Practical issues take center stage when the Sun and Mercury enter hardworking Virgo and your 10th House of Career on **August 22** and **23**. Concentrating on immediate tasks and refining your skills could raise your status on the job, but a lack of focus reduces your effectiveness.

KEEP IN MIND THIS MONTH

If you aspire to turn your life in a radical new direction, lay down a solid foundation with discipline and competence to create positive change.

KEY DATES

★ **AUGUST 4**
the amazing race
A fiery trine between the Sun in lively Leo and Uranus in audacious Aries stimulates your hunger for new experiences. You find yourself taking chances in pursuit of a good time and expressing your feelings in a more dramatic way thanks to this alignment of high-energy planets in your 9th House of Getaways and your 5th House of Fun and Games. Romantic feelings may be aroused when you push past personal limits and explore unfamiliar territory.

★ **AUGUST 7–9**
heroic efforts
Your high hopes, unreasonable fears, and strong opinions are out of proportion with reality on **August 7**, when giant Jupiter opposes potent Pluto. Yet going too far could stir up the passion you need to overcome obstacles. Fortunately, a highly creative Venus-Jupiter quintile on the **9th** sharpens

your imagination and can show you how to produce amazing results with limited resources. This quasi-magical aspect is also helpful for reestablishing your faith in the future of a relationship.

SUPER NOVA DAYS

★ **AUGUST 19–22**
embrace the unknown

Your patience runs out, along with your willingness to follow rules, on **August 19** when the Sun makes stressful aspects with Jupiter and Uranus. Rebellious feelings are not favorable for cooperation, but a breakthrough conversation, propelled by the futuristic Aquarius Full Moon in your 3rd House of Communication on the **20th**, could aim you in an exciting new direction. The high energy of the Jupiter-Uranus square on the **21st** intensifies when Mercury forms hard aspects to this planetary pair on the **22nd**. Brilliant insights pop out of thin air while your nerves are pulled taut by unexpected news. An overflow of information and last-minute deadlines creates tension and provokes verbal conflict. Adopting a flexible attitude allows you to learn something new without unraveling from the pressure.

★ **AUGUST 26–27**
guilty pleasures
Friends and colleagues may shock you when sweet Venus in your 11th House of Groups opposes disruptive Uranus on **August 26**. Switching up your plans, though, could make life more interesting. A greedy Venus-Jupiter square on the **27th** and raises expectations, challenging you to live up to your promises. Recognizing your true priorities helps you make the right choice instead of feeling like you have to satisfy everyone's needs.

★ **AUGUST 30**
partners in success
You are quick to spot great opportunities and notice talented people, enabling you to build efficient new alliances or successfully patch up old ones. A slick sextile between clever Mercury in your 10th House of Career with propitious Jupiter creates a perfect environment for making sound business decisions.

SEPTEMBER

TRUST IN THE PROCESS

It's the little things that count this month, especially when it comes to your career. September starts with the Sun and Mercury in detail-oriented Virgo and your professional 10th House, while the industrious Virgo New Moon on **September 5** encourages you to initiate training that can elevate your skills. Concentrating on a limited range of tasks may not be your idea of excitement, but narrowing your perspective now can broaden your opportunities for success and recognition later. Advantageous Jupiter and powerful Pluto align favorably with this Sun-Moon conjunction, attracting enthusiastic supporters and offering a strategic viewpoint that enables you to maximize your resources and make useful contacts. Collaborative conversations with friends and colleagues are likely when interactive Mercury moves into sociable Libra and your 11th House of Groups on **September 9**. However, promised cooperation may be slow to arrive once amicable Venus disappears into the shadows of Scorpio and your obscure 12th House on **September 11**.

You might be flooded with feelings when the supersensitive Pisces Full Moon illuminates your 4th House of Roots on **September 19**. Issues at home can distract you from your work, but this is also a gentle reminder that you need a refuge from your public responsibilities to find inner inspiration. The last of three subtle Saturn-Pluto sextiles on the **21st** can empower your dreams while also asking you to manage your resources more carefully. On the **22nd**, a little help from your friends arrives with the Sun's entry into congenial Libra and your 11th House of Groups, which marks the Autumn Equinox. But an imaginative Jupiter-Neptune sesquisquare on the **28th** that repeats on **December 17** and **June 11, 2014**, inflates your hopes with unrealistic fantasies.

KEEP IN MIND THIS MONTH

Approach your work like an apprentice, even if you have plenty of experience. You'll learn how to do a better job with less time and effort.

KEY DATES

★ **SEPTEMBER 7**
joy to the world
Your enthusiasm rises to a whole new level
when resilient Jupiter forms a heartwarming
sextile to the Sun, increasing your confidence
and allowing your generosity to shine.
Having fun with friends or volunteering for
a cause can fill you with deep satisfaction.
Additionally, a creative Mercury-Jupiter
quintile stimulates your curiosity and helps
you find the information you need to solve a
tricky problem.

★ **SEPTEMBER 9–11**
addition by subtraction
The harder you push, the more resistance you
meet on **September 9**, when aggressive Mars in
your 9th House of Big Ideas squares controlling
Saturn. Travel delays and educational setbacks
are possible, though you might be able to avoid
them by planning in advance and creating a
less ambitious schedule. Doing one thing well
is better than overloading your days with too

many activities. Failing to focus your efforts produces additional pressures and potential power struggles on the **11th**, when punishing Pluto quincunxes Mars. Productivity falters and frustration follows unless you're able to set aside distractions and deal with one tough task at a time.

SUPER NOVA DAYS

★ **SEPTEMBER 14–17**
agent of change
A lack of support from peers dampens your mood on **September 14**, when Mercury forms a tense square with manipulative Pluto. Yet if you dig more deeply into the situation, you may recognize that you're not heading in the right direction. Happily, experimenting with innovative methods can produce surprisingly positive results as courageous Mars trines avant-garde Uranus in your 5th House of Creativity. You might either persuade others to accept your unusual ideas—or be convinced that someone else is mentally off track—with an intellectually charged Mercury-Uranus opposition on the **16th**. If you can stay cool

and remain on point, a smart Mercury-Mars sextile on the **17th** clears the air, enhancing cooperation and increasing productivity.

★ **SEPTEMBER 19**
too many cooks
A gregarious Mercury-Jupiter square offers too much input today, and your mind may shut off from any more noise. Conversely, overexplaining yourself can be equally dissuasive to others. More information doesn't lead to understanding, so try to boil your position down to a few key points that are easier to digest. A diversity of perspectives is stimulating, yet you can't make wise decisions if you take everyone's opinions into account.

★ **SEPTEMBER 26**
pleasant surprise
A juicy trine between loving Venus and ebullient Jupiter offers delight in even the dreariest circumstances. Asking for what you need in a nondemanding manner produces positive reactions when you might least expect them.

OCTOBER

ELEMENT OF SURPRISE

Your interactions with others are off the wall
this month with the ambiguous Libra New
Moon falling in your 11th House of Groups on
October 4. The harmony associated with Libra
can be unsettled by mistrust and manipulation
as it runs into some rough waters choppy with
surprises. Unpredictable Uranus's opposition
to this Sun-Moon conjunction and stressful
squares from secretive Pluto and judgmental
Jupiter can complicate almost any gathering.
Graciously adjusting to changes in alliances and
breakdowns in cooperation reduces risks, while
adapting to shifts in collective goals could create
unexpected opportunities. Your eagerness to
take risks catches the attention of others when
Venus enters adventurous Sagittarius on the
7th. But don't let vanity and personal matters
push work completely out of the picture, because
enterprising Mars enters conscientious Virgo
and your 10th House of Career on **October 15**.
Initiating projects and dedicating yourself to do
the best job possible can garner you recognition—
or at least avoid weakening your position.

The impetuous Aries Full Moon Lunar Eclipse on **October 18** in your 5th House of Romance, Children, and Creativity tempts you to leap without looking. Engaging in new forms of fun and self-expression is fine if you don't upset friends and colleagues by ignoring their concerns. Mercury begins a three-week retrograde cycle in enigmatic Scorpio and your 12th House of Privacy on the **21st**, a move that slows down the flow of information and may even cause you to misplace messages. However, this is also a great time to explore the mysteries of metaphysics or the depths of your psyche if you are so inclined. The Sun's entry into Scorpio on the **23rd** underscores how important it is that you work quietly behind the scenes until it's your time to shine.

KEEP IN MIND THIS MONTH

If frustration makes it too difficult for you to get along with others, working independently until the dust settles may be your best move.

KEY DATES

★ **OCTOBER 1–3**
be the change
The Sun's move from a complex square
with Pluto on **October 1** to an explosive
opposition to Uranus on the **3rd** could push
you to a breaking point. If you're dealing with
unrelenting pressure from an unreasonable
individual, you could be tempted to suddenly
end the relationship. A more desirable story
is one where you gain more power in an
organization, which you then use to radically
alter the structure of the group.

★ **OCTOBER 7**
honest to a fault
You're ready to play and might even create
some mischief with an itchy Mars-Uranus
sesquisquare and tantalizing Venus entering
your 1st House of Personality. It's all too easy
to lower your guard and express yourself with
disturbing honesty. Of course, you might just
be teasing, but that's not necessarily obvious
to everyone else. Make sure your signals are

clear so that people know whether you're just having fun or are finally getting something off your chest by speaking the truth.

SUPER NOVA DAYS

★ **OCTOBER 11–12**
pushing the envelope
Your lust for life knows few bounds as fun-loving Venus in Sagittarius forms an unbalanced sesquisquare with expansive Jupiter on **October 11**. You may be ready to take a chance on love, but your evaluation of its costs may be off base. Seeking unusual ways to enjoy yourself makes sense as long as you avoid overestimating someone and underestimating the consequences of risky behavior. Your unbridled enthusiasm, though, is likely to continue on the **12th** with an unwieldy Sun-Jupiter square, yet your careless remarks and brash behavior could alienate a person close to you. It's fine to express your opinions as long as they're tempered by a healthy dose of sensitivity to the beliefs of others.

★ **OCTOBER 16**
anything goes
A sassy trine from Venus in your 1st House of Personality to Uranus in your 5th House of Creativity encourages you to experiment with your appearance. Switching up your style makes your day more fun and attracts a good deal of attention. Of course, your provocative behavior will make you even more intriguing to others. Luckily, you should be able to have a blast breaking a few social rules without getting into too much trouble.

★ **OCTOBER 24**
proceed with caution
A tendency to go into hard-sell mode doesn't necessarily help your cause on **October 24**. It's not easy for you to keep your enthusiasm in check with a hyperactive Mars-Jupiter semisquare, but taking your foot off the gas once in a while will make everyone feel safer.

NOVEMBER

OUT OF THE SHADOWS

This is a transitional month when spending time completing unfinished business will free you to start on your next big adventure. The recurring Uranus-Pluto square on **November 1** can leave you questioning a previous financial decision, but looking back with regret is not your style. Nevertheless, an intense Scorpio Solar Eclipse on **November 3** may force you to confront issues you don't want to face. This eclipse occurs in your 12th House of Endings and joins sobering Saturn to push you up against uncomfortable realities. However, if you're willing to do the hard work of honestly addressing your doubts and tackling your obligations, you can build an inner strength that carries you far into the future. Managing your resources carefully is the message of value-conscious Venus's entry into stingy Capricorn and your 2nd House of Self-Worth on the **5th**. Exercising financial discipline, investing in the right tools, and developing your talents pays dividends if you're patient and persistent. Your visionary ruling planet, Jupiter, turns retrograde on **November 7**, requiring reflection and, perhaps, readjustment of long-range plans. While the big picture may be fuzzy, communicative Mercury's forward shift on the **10th** is great for catching up on details during the days ahead.

Spiritual Neptune's direct shift in your 4th House of Roots on **November 13** revives old dreams and brings more imagination into your household. However, you still must handle mundane matters and deal with boring routines with the steadfast Taurus Full Moon illuminating your 6th House of Work on the **17th**. On **November 21**, the Sun emerges from the shadows of your 12th House and enters your enthusiastic sign. A boost of energy and optimism comes with this solar shift into your 1st House of Personality, where your effervescent charisma and confidence cast you in the spotlight for everyone to admire.

KEEP IN MIND THIS MONTH

It's not easy to let go of unrealizable fantasies and move on from regret, but this emotional process creates fertile soil in which you can grow new dreams.

KEY DATES

★ **NOVEMBER 6**
attitude adjustment
You may feel constrained, frustrated, or ignored with the Sun's conjunction to repressive Saturn in your 12th House of Obscurity. It's critical to avoid getting bogged down in regret or resentment; focus on possible constructive actions instead. Taking responsibility for your situation is an excellent way to empower yourself with faith and discipline, which is vastly preferable to undermining reactions of guilt, shame, or blame.

★ **NOVEMBER 12**
sunshine on your shoulders
You receive the nurturing support of a caring ally today—and, with it, a rising tide of hope. The Sun harmoniously trines generous Jupiter in your 8th House of Deep Sharing, bringing light into the darker parts of your mind. A partner, colleague, or friend provides encouragement by recognizing abilities or accomplishments that

are usually underappreciated. It may take time to ride this wave all the way to the shores of success, but at least you can feel that you're on your way to a better place.

★ **NOVEMBER 19–20**
get smart
A sextile from dynamic Mars in your 10th House of Career to jovial Jupiter in your 8th House of Joint Ventures supplies the impetus for tackling team projects on **November 19**. Planning ahead, though, takes you further than simply working as diligently as you can. Mercury's messy quincunx with unruly Uranus on the **20th** can distract you with irrelevant ideas and quirky conversations. Fortunately, your focus returns later in the day when Mercury sextiles laserlike Pluto, putting your mind back on track.

SUPER NOVA DAYS

★ **NOVEMBER 24–25**
lost and found
Your spirit soars when the Sagittarius Sun squares phantasmagoric Neptune on

November 24. While your heart may open with compassion and images of a better tomorrow, your chronic tendency to overlook details can lead to costly decisions. With a romantically foolish Venus-Neptune semisquare on the **25th**, you continue losing sight of practical considerations in a fog of fantasies. Enjoying delicious moments of escapism is delightful as long as you don't build your entire future on them. Mercury's conjunction to no-nonsense Saturn will quickly tear away the veils of illusion and demand that you face the simple facts.

★ **NOVEMBER 28**
sweet spot
Applying a bit of common sense helps you seize today's opportunities for more money, love, and pleasure and bring them within reach. The caution of Venus in conservative Capricorn encounters temptations that are hard to resist when it opposes jocular Jupiter. However, the practical wisdom of a Mercury-Jupiter trine allows you to recognize any errors of judgment and quickly correct them.

DECEMBER

COUNT YOUR BLESSINGS

Reevaluating major plans and projects adds a useful dose of pragmatism to this joyous holiday season. Farsighted Jupiter's favorable trine with strategic Saturn on **December 12** gives you a chance to review decisions you've made since their first trine on **July 17** and adjust them as needed to reach your goals before their final alignment on **May 24, 2014**. You could, however, act impulsively with the flamboyant Sagittarius New Moon in your 1st House of Personality on **December 2**. Breaking free of old habits to discover new approaches to creativity, play, and romance comes naturally with unorthodox Uranus's trine to this lunation. Ideas start flowing more readily, encouraging you to become more outspoken and willing to discuss your aspirations openly when talkative Mercury enters Sagittarius on the **4th**. You're likely to find the Winged Messenger's visit to your sign delightful, but sensitive individuals may respond better to more discreet discussions.

Nerves are running rampant when the frisky Gemini Full Moon brightens your 7th House of

Partners on **December 17**. Uranus the Awakener turns direct on the same day, attracting unconventional and sometimes unstable people. Yet this lunation also enables you to see relationships in a different light and increases your options for ways to connect with others. The Winter Solstice arrives on **December 21** with the Sun's entry into traditional Capricorn and your 2nd House of Income. You don't want to be like Scrooge, but taking your economic situation more seriously is wise, nonetheless. Venus turns retrograde in your resourceful 2nd House, also on the **21st**, reminding you that reorganizing finances and questioning your values can help you improve your cash flow.

KEEP IN MIND THIS MONTH

Setting aside time for serious thought about your future may be the best present you can give to yourself and those you love.

KEY DATES

★ **DECEMBER 6–7**
wearing rose-colored glasses
A fuzzy Mercury-Neptune square on
December 6 encourages idealization that
can make you see and hear what you want
to believe rather than experiencing things as
they really are. This hopeful illusion feeds
your imagination but can lead to confusing
conversations and misstatements of facts. An
unbalanced Mercury-Jupiter sesquisquare
continues this pattern on the **7th**, amplifying
your tendency toward exaggeration. Happily,
assertive Mars's entry into accommodating
Libra provides the diplomatic skills necessary
to alleviate awkward situations.

★ **DECEMBER 9–10**
smooth operator
Thanks to a brilliant Mars-Jupiter quintile
on **December 9**, you seem like a magician
for getting incompatible people to work well
together. But a wayward Sun-Jupiter quincunx
on the **10th** tempts you to press your luck

and expect everyone to go along with your plans. If you take on unreliable partners or stretch your credibility by promising too much, an ingenious Mercury-Uranus trine reveals innovative ways to get you out of a jam.

★ **DECEMBER 16**

consider your audience

It's fun to be funny and people love to laugh, but your sense of humor could rub some the wrong way today. Mischievous Mercury in carefree Sagittarius is entangled in a clunky quincunx with Jupiter in touchy Cancer and your 8th House of Intimacy. Even if there's truth in what you say, tailor your message to those around you to avoid embarrassment and be less controversial.

★ **DECEMBER 25**

chaotic christmas

You might be eager to have an exciting holiday—but this one is unlikely to unfold as planned. Impatient Mars in your 11th House of Groups opposes shocking Uranus in your 5th House of Self-Expression, which can spring

surprises and trigger explosive reactions
from uncooperative individuals. You may be
unabashedly bored by the predictable family
rituals that you've done so many times before.
Celebrating in new and unusual ways puts an
unexpected spin on the day's activities and
calms your restless feelings.

SUPER NOVA DAYS

★ **DECEMBER 29–31**
   mind games
   Your patience for compromise is limited
   as mental Mercury and the Sun in your
   2nd House of Income slam into a square
   with erratic Uranus on **December 29–30**.
   Conversations about your finances may
   suddenly veer off in odd directions, breaking
   down ordinary patterns of perception and
   leaving you uncertain about your future. An
   intense Mars-Pluto square on the **30th** incites
   fear and mistrust, which may be amplified
   when analytical Mercury aspects both planets
   on the **31st**. Nevertheless, if you can articulate
   your concerns clearly, you might just be on
   your way to resolving a financial problem.

APPENDIXES

★

2013 MONTH AT-A-GLANCE
ASTROCALENDAR

★

FAMOUS SAGITTARIANS

★

SAGITTARIUS IN LOVE

TUESDAY 1

WEDNESDAY 2

THURSDAY 3

FRIDAY 4 ★ Your enthusiasm may motivate you to oversell or overreach

SATURDAY 5 ★

SUNDAY 6

MONDAY 7

TUESDAY 8

WEDNESDAY 9

THURSDAY 10

FRIDAY 11 ★ ● Choose one path to your goal and stick to it

SATURDAY 12

SUNDAY 13

MONDAY 14 ★ Good intentions may not be enough

TUESDAY 15

WEDNESDAY 16

THURSDAY 17

FRIDAY 18

SATURDAY 19

SUNDAY 20

MONDAY 21

TUESDAY 22 ★ Keep all channels of communication open

WEDNESDAY 23

THURSDAY 24

FRIDAY 25 ★ **SUPER NOVA DAYS** Your powers of persuasion are strong

SATURDAY 26 ★ ○

SUNDAY 27

MONDAY 28

TUESDAY 29

WEDNESDAY 30

THURSDAY 31

★ designates key date

FRIDAY 1

SATURDAY 2

SUNDAY 3

MONDAY 4 ★ Show tenderness to those you love

TUESDAY 5

WEDNESDAY 6 ★ **SUPER NOVA DAYS** Promote your ideas and act with enthusiasm

THURSDAY 7 ★

FRIDAY 8 ★

SATURDAY 9 ★

SUNDAY 10 ★ ●

MONDAY 11

TUESDAY 12

WEDNESDAY 13

THURSDAY 14

FRIDAY 15 ★ Anger can be converted into positive action

SATURDAY 16 ★

SUNDAY 17

MONDAY 18

TUESDAY 19

WEDNESDAY 20

THURSDAY 21 ★ You may be wistful about the past

FRIDAY 22

SATURDAY 23

SUNDAY 24

MONDAY 25 ★ O Don't waste time getting caught up in petty arguments

TUESDAY 26 ★

WEDNESDAY 27

THURSDAY 28

FRIDAY 1	
SATURDAY 2	
SUNDAY 3	
MONDAY 4 ★	Maintain your moral compass
TUESDAY 5	
WEDNESDAY 6	
THURSDAY 7 ★	Careless speech could create expectations you cannot meet
FRIDAY 8 ★	
SATURDAY 9 ★	
SUNDAY 10	
MONDAY 11 ●	
TUESDAY 12	
WEDNESDAY 13	
THURSDAY 14	
FRIDAY 15	
SATURDAY 16 ★	Find answers in unexpected places
SUNDAY 17	
MONDAY 18	
TUESDAY 19	
WEDNESDAY 20	
THURSDAY 21	
FRIDAY 22 ★	Innovation and spontaneity are strong
SATURDAY 23 ★	
SUNDAY 24	
MONDAY 25	
TUESDAY 26	
WEDNESDAY 27 ○	
THURSDAY 28 ★	**SUPER NOVA DAYS** Experiment with your attitude
FRIDAY 29 ★	
SATURDAY 30 ★	
SUNDAY 31 ★	

MONDAY 1 ★ You can impress others easily today

TUESDAY 2

WEDNESDAY 3

THURSDAY 4

FRIDAY 5

SATURDAY 6 ★ What you see is not what you get

SUNDAY 7 ★

MONDAY 8 ★

TUESDAY 9

WEDNESDAY 10 ●

THURSDAY 11

FRIDAY 12

SATURDAY 13

SUNDAY 14 ★ Fix mistakes and correct misunderstandings

MONDAY 15 ★

TUESDAY 16

WEDNESDAY 17

THURSDAY 18

FRIDAY 19

SATURDAY 20 ★ **SUPER NOVA DAYS** You might feel like you can do anything

SUNDAY 21 ★

MONDAY 22

TUESDAY 23

WEDNESDAY 24

THURSDAY 25 ○

FRIDAY 26

SATURDAY 27

SUNDAY 28 ★ There's little room for error today

MONDAY 29

TUESDAY 30

WEDNESDAY 1

THURSDAY 2 ★ Making mountains out of molehills is not very productive

FRIDAY 3

SATURDAY 4

SUNDAY 5

MONDAY 6

TUESDAY 7 ★ Focus on the task at hand now

WEDNESDAY 8

THURSDAY 9 ●

FRIDAY 10

SATURDAY 11

SUNDAY 12

MONDAY 13 ★ Don't make any serious commitments

TUESDAY 14 ★

WEDNESDAY 15 ★

THURSDAY 16

FRIDAY 17

SATURDAY 18

SUNDAY 19

MONDAY 20

TUESDAY 21

WEDNESDAY 22

THURSDAY 23

FRIDAY 24 ★ Enjoy light-hearted play today

SATURDAY 25 ○

SUNDAY 26

MONDAY 27 ★ **SUPER NOVA DAYS** Your words have greater impact now

TUESDAY 28 ★

WEDNESDAY 29

THURSDAY 30

FRIDAY 31

SATURDAY 1 ★ Strange encounters are to be expected today

SUNDAY 2

MONDAY 3

TUESDAY 4

WEDNESDAY 5

THURSDAY 6

FRIDAY 7 ★ Avoid rushing into agreements

SATURDAY 8 ★ ●

SUNDAY 9

MONDAY 10

TUESDAY 11

WEDNESDAY 12

THURSDAY 13

FRIDAY 14

SATURDAY 15

SUNDAY 16

MONDAY 17 ★ SUPER NOVA DAYS Toss caution to the wind

TUESDAY 18 ★

WEDNESDAY 19 ★

THURSDAY 20

FRIDAY 21

SATURDAY 22

SUNDAY 23 ○

MONDAY 24

TUESDAY 25

WEDNESDAY 26

THURSDAY 27 ★ Buckle down and meet your responsibilities

FRIDAY 28 ★

SATURDAY 29

SUNDAY 30

MONDAY 1 ★ Wait until things settle down before making your move

TUESDAY 2 ★

WEDNESDAY 3 ★

THURSDAY 4 ★

FRIDAY 5

SATURDAY 6

SUNDAY 7

MONDAY 8 ●

TUESDAY 9 ★ Listen carefully to others

WEDNESDAY 10

THURSDAY 11

FRIDAY 12

SATURDAY 13 ★ Use a bit of self-restraint today

SUNDAY 14

MONDAY 15

TUESDAY 16

WEDNESDAY 17

THURSDAY 18

FRIDAY 19 ★ **SUPER NOVA DAYS** Your dreams seem more real than ever

SATURDAY 20 ★

SUNDAY 21 ★

MONDAY 22 ★ ○

TUESDAY 23

WEDNESDAY 24

THURSDAY 25

FRIDAY 26

SATURDAY 27 ★ Slowing down can produce a sweet outcome

SUNDAY 28 ★

MONDAY 29

TUESDAY 30

WEDNESDAY 31

THURSDAY 1

FRIDAY 2

SATURDAY 3

SUNDAY 4 ★ Push past personal limits and explore unfamiliar territory

MONDAY 5

TUESDAY 6 ●

WEDNESDAY 7 ★ Reestablish your faith in the future of a relationship

THURSDAY 8 ★

FRIDAY 9 ★

SATURDAY 10

SUNDAY 11

MONDAY 12

TUESDAY 13

WEDNESDAY 14

THURSDAY 15

FRIDAY 16

SATURDAY 17

SUNDAY 18

MONDAY 19 ★ SUPER NOVA DAYS Embrace the unknown

TUESDAY 20 ★ ○

WEDNESDAY 21 ★

THURSDAY 22 ★

FRIDAY 23

SATURDAY 24

SUNDAY 25

MONDAY 26 ★ Live up to your promises

TUESDAY 27 ★

WEDNESDAY 28

THURSDAY 29

FRIDAY 30 ★ You are quick to spot great opportunities

SATURDAY 31

SUNDAY 1	
MONDAY 2	
TUESDAY 3	
WEDNESDAY 4	
THURSDAY 5	●
FRIDAY 6	
SATURDAY 7 ★	Allow your generosity to shine

SUNDAY 8	
MONDAY 9 ★	Pushing hard only increases resistance

TUESDAY 10 ★	
WEDNESDAY 11 ★	
THURSDAY 12	
FRIDAY 13	
SATURDAY 14 ★	**SUPER NOVA DAYS** Experiment with innovative methods

SUNDAY 15 ★	
MONDAY 16 ★	
TUESDAY 17 ★	
WEDNESDAY 18	
THURSDAY 19 ★	O Boil your position down to a few key points

FRIDAY 20	
SATURDAY 21	
SUNDAY 22	
MONDAY 23	
TUESDAY 24	
WEDNESDAY 25	
THURSDAY 26 ★	Ask for what you need in a non-demanding manner

FRIDAY 27	
SATURDAY 28	
SUNDAY 29	
MONDAY 30	

TUESDAY 1 ★ Be the change you want to see in the world

WEDNESDAY 2 ★

THURSDAY 3 ★

FRIDAY 4 ●

SATURDAY 5

SUNDAY 6

MONDAY 7 ★ Make sure that your signals are clear

TUESDAY 8

WEDNESDAY 9

THURSDAY 10

FRIDAY 11 ★ **SUPER NOVA DAYS** Take a chance on love

SATURDAY 12 ★

SUNDAY 13

MONDAY 14

TUESDAY 15

WEDNESDAY 16 ★ Switching up your style attracts attention

THURSDAY 17

FRIDAY 18 ○

SATURDAY 19

SUNDAY 20

MONDAY 21

TUESDAY 22

WEDNESDAY 23

THURSDAY 24 ★ Proceed with caution today

FRIDAY 25

SATURDAY 26

SUNDAY 27

MONDAY 28

TUESDAY 29

WEDNESDAY 30

THURSDAY 31

FRIDAY 1	
SATURDAY 2	
SUNDAY 3	●
MONDAY 4	
TUESDAY 5	
WEDNESDAY 6	★ Take responsibility for your actions

THURSDAY 7	
FRIDAY 8	
SATURDAY 9	
SUNDAY 10	
MONDAY 11	
TUESDAY 12	★ A rising tide of hope provides encouragement

WEDNESDAY 13	
THURSDAY 14	
FRIDAY 15	
SATURDAY 16	
SUNDAY 17	○
MONDAY 18	
TUESDAY 19	★ Planning ahead takes you further than working hard

WEDNESDAY 20	★
THURSDAY 21	
FRIDAY 22	
SATURDAY 23	
SUNDAY 24	★ **SUPER NOVA DAYS** Your heart opens with compassion

MONDAY 25	★
TUESDAY 26	
WEDNESDAY 27	
THURSDAY 28	★ Common sense helps you seize opportunities

| FRIDAY 29 | |
| SATURDAY 30 | |

SUNDAY 1	
MONDAY 2	●
TUESDAY 3	
WEDNESDAY 4	
THURSDAY 5	
FRIDAY 6 ★	You see and hear what you want to believe
SATURDAY 7 ★	
SUNDAY 8	
MONDAY 9 ★	An innovative solution gets you out of a jam
TUESDAY 10 ★	
WEDNESDAY 11	
THURSDAY 12	
FRIDAY 13	
SATURDAY 14	
SUNDAY 15	
MONDAY 16 ★	Consider you audience
TUESDAY 17	○
WEDNESDAY 18	
THURSDAY 19	
FRIDAY 20	
SATURDAY 21	
SUNDAY 22	
MONDAY 23	
TUESDAY 24	
WEDNESDAY 25 ★	Celebrate in new and unusual ways
THURSDAY 26	
FRIDAY 27	
SATURDAY 28	
SUNDAY 29 ★	**SUPER NOVA DAYS** Your patience for compromise is limited
MONDAY 30 ★	
TUESDAY 31 ★	

FAMOUS SAGITTARIANS

Billie Jean King	★	11/22/1943
Rodney Dangerfield	★	11/22/1921
Jamie Lee Curtis	★	11/22/1958
Boris Karloff	★	11/23/1887
Billy the Kid	★	11/23/1859
Harpo Marx	★	11/23/1888
Scott Joplin	★	11/24/1868
John F. Kennedy, Jr.	★	11/25/1960
Joe DiMaggio	★	11/25/1914
Tina Turner	★	11/26/1939
Charles Schulz	★	11/26/1922
Caroline Kennedy	★	11/27/1957
Bruce Lee	★	11/27/1940
Jimi Hendrix	★	11/27/1942
Berry Gordy, Jr.	★	11/28/1929
Jon Stewart	★	11/28/1962
Louisa May Alcott	★	11/29/1832
C. S. Lewis	★	11/29/1898
Billy Idol	★	11/30/1955
Mark Twain	★	11/30/1835
Dick Clark	★	11/30/1929
Winston Churchill	★	11/30/1874
Bette Midler	★	12/1/1945
Woody Allen	★	12/1/1935
Richard Pryor	★	12/1/1940
Lucy Liu	★	12/2/1968
Gianni Versace	★	12/2/1946
Britney Spears	★	12/2/1981
Daryl Hannah	★	12/3/1960
Jean-Luc Godard	★	12/3/1930
Ozzy Osbourne	★	12/3/1948
Jay-Z	★	12/4/1970
Marisa Tomei	★	12/4/1964
Tyra Banks	★	12/4/1973
Walt Disney	★	12/5/1901
Little Richard	★	12/5/1932
Larry Bird	★	12/7/1956

FAMOUS SAGITTARIANS

Sinéad O'Connor	★	12/8/1966
Jim Morrison	★	12/8/1943
Sammy Davis, Jr.	★	12/8/1925
Diego Rivera	★	12/8/1886
Judi Dench	★	12/9/1934
John Malkovich	★	12/9/1953
Donny Osmond	★	12/9/1957
Emily Dickinson	★	12/10/1830
Rita Moreno	★	12/11/1931
John Kerry	★	12/11/1943
Jennifer Connelly	★	12/12/1970
Frank Sinatra	★	12/12/1915
Jamie Foxx	★	12/13/1967
Ted Nugent	★	12/13/1948
Patty Duke	★	12/14/1946
Nostradamus	★	12/14/1503
Shirley Jackson	★	12/14/1919
Jane Austen	★	12/16/1775
Ludwig van Beethoven	★	12/17/1770
William Safire	★	12/17/1929
Brad Pitt	★	12/18/1963
Betty Grable	★	12/18/1916
Ty Cobb	★	12/18/1886
Ossie Davis	★	12/18/1917
Keith Richards	★	12/18/1943
Christina Aguilera	★	12/18/1980
Steven Spielberg	★	12/18/1946
Cicely Tyson	★	12/19/1933
Frank Zappa	★	12/21/1940
Jane Fonda	★	12/21/1937
Florence Griffith Joyner	★	12/21/1959
Kiefer Sutherland	★	12/21/1966

SAGITTARIUS IN LOVE

SAGITTARIUS & ARIES (MARCH 21–APRIL 19)

You project optimism and are attracted to the big picture with larger-than-life ambitions. Usually you are friendly, humorous, and even inspirational at times. You seem to be lucky and often meet end results with success. All this adds up to you being a great match for pioneering Aries who, with good cheer and amicable intention, sometimes loses interest half way through a project. The Ram benefits from your goal-orientation, but you get some goodies from your Aries lover, too. He or she motivates you to get going. Together you two fire signs can pave a path of inspiration and creativity. You'll engage in all kinds of activities together, including travel, sports, and socializing. Although you get along well, you're both so independent that you may not be willing to commit to a long-term relationship, unless you have the Moon or Mars in an earth sign or a water sign. Although you like adventure, your Aries lover may need more excitement than you'd like and can annoy you with his or her "I-want-it-my-way" attitude. Even so, you find a playmate in Aries and if you can keep your feet on the ground, you'll make a joyous couple.

SAGITTARIUS & TAURUS (APRIL 20–MAY 20)

You want to dream up a plan with far-reaching goals and then use it as a blueprint for the adventure that others call life. You're restless, with a strong yearning for faraway places and new ideas. As such, you love to travel—in the real world or in your mind. Archers often pursue fulfilling careers in fields that allow them movement and versatility. Although your stable, loyal Taurus makes a good companion, there are significant differences of style between you. You're not satisfied with the status quo. Your Taurus lover likes things the way they are, especially if they're comfortable. Taurus will provide you with practical advice and rewarding friendship. You, on the other hand, can help your sometimes lazy Bull move into action and become more interested in social affairs. Romantically, you may be more athletic, compared to your partner's simple sensual indulgence. If you have the Moon or Mars in an earth or water sign, you will find it easier to get along with your Bull, for you'll be more comfortable in the realm of the senses. Regardless of other planetary indicators, this union can create a solid foundation for you. Get past your resistance to becoming more stable and together you can make a good team and create a solid love life.

SAGITTARIUS & GEMINI (MAY 21–JUNE 20)

Opposites sometimes do attract, and you and your Gemini lover are opposite each other in the zodiac circle. Both of you emphasize communication and education, and prefer to be active, versatile, and spontaneous. You, however, have a wider reach in your vision and loftier goals than your Gemini lover, who stays closer to home, both physically and mentally. Your exalted vision and global perspective expands into cultures far and wide, and you probably have airline mileage to prove it. You partner's travel, however, is inclined to be more like commuting on a day-to-day basis within the structure of his or her daily life. You may discover that your partner gets on your nerves because Geminis always seem to be talking, even when he or she has nothing important to say. If, however, you have Venus or Mars in an air sign, you'll be less judgmental of Gemini's tendency to waste energy in endless communication. Ultimately, your fire mixes well with your partner's air. You each add a perspective that the other lacks. You make a great work or play team, but you can be a little scattered, so at least one of you should maintain a solid footing in your affairs. Playful and alive, you can certainly spark chemistry between you.

SAGITTARIUS & CANCER (JUNE 21–JULY 22)

Your restless nature and inquiring spirit may be a
bit unsettling for the more home-centered, passive
Cancer. You can't stay in one place very long before
you get this irrepressible need to expand your
horizons and to go out exploring unknown vistas.
Meanwhile, your Cancer lover requires a safe
haven where he or she feels securely protected
from the tides of change. If your Crab is able to
give you the freedom to explore the outer reaches,
you may find a nurturing friend and a tender lover.
But it is also possible that you will feel trapped by
the emotional insecurities of your Cancer mate.
It may be beyond your capabilities to give your
lover what he or she needs—you're committed to
truthful, straightforward behaviors, which may
hurt the Crab's overly sensitive feelings. If the
Moon or Mars in your chart is in a water sign, then
you'll probably be more responsive to your Cancer
partner's emotional needs. You must find ways
to comfort the Crab's worries. Additionally, he or
she must be willing to include your sense of global
awareness within the home and in the family.
This is not a natural pairing, but together you
can create a stable home from which to journey
outward, both in body and in spirit.

SAGITTARIUS & LEO (JULY 23–AUGUST 22)

You can be philosophical as you point the arrow of your thoughts toward future adventures and far off places. Like you, Leo is an action-oriented fire sign. The Lion can be generous and love to play as much as you do. When it turns romantic with a Leo, the skies open, the seas part, and magic happens. Give your Lion ample attention and he or she will blaze a trail of dreams with you. Leos love going out on the town, creative arts, and playful excursions of most any type. These traits complement your sense of adventure—the two of you enjoy your mutual companionship a great deal. You're both outgoing and expressive, so others may see the two of you as a dynamic duo. Romantic chemistry is strong, that is until the Leo's ego is bruised by your attention to some travel destination that doesn't involve your mate. You don't understand this side of your Leo, because your need for approval isn't as strong. Vulnerable Leo needs a lot more affirmation than you do. Luckly, though, neither of you holds a grudge or builds resentment, unless you have the Moon or Mars in a water or earth sign. You're quite compatible with your Leo, and together you'll engage life to the fullest, with a lot of fun along the way.

SAGITTARIUS & VIRGO (AUGUST 23–SEPT. 22)

You are good-natured, high-spirited, and present a solid public image. Your superior abilities in higher learning are attractive to Virgos, who are more image-conscious than they'd like to admit. While you like the big picture, they're focused on the minute details: you admire a forest; they're in awe of a leaf's veins. They're quite critical, which may not be to your liking. You and your Virgo lover can work well if you learn to appreciate each other's unique traits. Your enthusiasm can inspire Virgo to reach for the stars, and your dry humor can help them lighten their critical touch. Beneath the cool exterior, your Virgo partner is quite witty, and he or she will enjoy your playful teasing and candor. You'll dream up fantastic adventures, and Virgo will offer you rational advice. If you have the Moon or Mars in an earth sign, you'll be better equipped to take the criticism in a constructive manner. You may be very attracted to Virgo's mind or refined beauty, but this relationship may lack the tender vulnerability that adds depth to an intimate relationship. You'll have to work toward expressing your feelings. This is a well-meaning union that can be successful, especially if you share work interests or a common philosophical outlook on life.

SAGITTARIUS & LIBRA (SEPT. 23–OCT. 22)

You love to socialize. At a party, you'll be one of the people who appears confident and is having a good time. You appreciate refined tastes and open-minded attitudes. Libra makes an aesthetically pleasing companion for you, as both of you are attracted to art, theater, music, and uplifting surroundings. You attract a wide variety of friendships, and prefer to keep the company of those with similar values and tastes. Your Libra partner has a natural talent to put you at ease, for he or she is gracious and tends to your needs and the needs of the relationship in a loving and caring manner. Your occasional blunt mannerism can ruffle the feathers of Libra's fine social protocol. On the other hand, you just may not understand why your Libra puts so much stock into the rules of proper social etiquette. You're a hands-on person, while your mate can be satisfied talking about it rather than doing it. If you have Venus or Mars in an air sign, it can increase your acceptance of this difference. If you choose to live together, your home will be filled with books, art, and travel maps. Ultimately, the two of you are compatible enough that you can overcome whatever obstacles come between you.

SAGITTARIUS & SCORPIO (OCT. 23–NOV. 21)

You Archers are quite resourceful and able to gather whatever you need for projects and goals. You make fine teachers, life-long students, and can excel in politics or law. Scorpios are cosmically programmed to delve into situations with a keen ability to solve problems. They are attracted to your big thinking and may be inspired by your philosophical ideas. Together, you can enjoy mutual studies, movies, and discussing world events. You will need to share common interests, as other areas of your relationship may be more difficult because of how differently you view life. You're basically optimistic and always see the brighter side of a situation. Your Scorpio partner may perceive this Pollyanna-type behavior as naïve. He or she wants to wallow around in the darker side of affairs. Scorpios aren't necessarily pessimistic; they just don't like glossing over unpleasantness. If you have Venus in Scorpio or the Moon in any water sign, you may be more open to your mate's intense feelings. Together, you may be able to cultivate each other's hidden talents. No matter what else, you'll have to ensure that your Scorpio lover feels like he or she is being heard. Trust and shared interests are the keys to success.

SAGITTARIUS & SAGITTARIUS (NOV. 22–DEC. 21)

When you look into the mirror of relationships and hook up with another Archer, you are initially delighted to have found such a cheerful and good-humored soul. After all, both of you are high-minded, restless, and adventurous. And, of course, you're fun to be with. Put two of you together and it sounds awesome. You scurry around biking, hiking, and running from place to place. You have long talks about philosophical ideas, world religions, and educational pursuits. You make the best of friends. Problems can arise, however, when you try to settle into a mutually satisfying routine. Neither of you is inclined to provide the stability that the relationship needs. You'll both be coming and going, sometimes together but often without the other in tow, since your interests will diverge and neither of you will want to give up your independence. But if one or both of you have Venus in Capricorn or Scorpio, or the Moon in any earth sign, the chances for long-term compatibility are greatly improved. If the two of you can slow down long enough to make a commitment to live and love together, your home may still look like a hotel room! Aside from the love you share, your strong friendship can hold your union together.

SAGITTARIUS & CAPRICORN (DEC. 22–JAN. 19)

Archers can get uncomfortable if life becomes too serious and mundane. When you meet up with Capricorns, you're confronted with how serious and responsible they are by nature. This can get old, as you may feel that your Capricorn partner is often raining on your parade, telling you that your plans to go to India in June and your Kenyan photography trip are impractical. He or she is probably right, but you don't want to hear it. You're usually willing to risk your security for the sake of adventure, while your partner would rather pay the bills before embarking on a journey. On the positive side, your Goat can help you with managing practical matters, like finance. It may not be as much fun as you'd prefer, but you'll probably have the money to actually go on that safari you've always dreamed about. You have a positive influence on hard-working Capricorn as you bring laughter and lightness into his or her life. Although Goats are serious about work, they also take love seriously, too. If you have Venus in Capricorn or if your Moon is in any earth sign, your chances for compatibility are improved, as is the likelihood of sexual chemistry. When the two of you decide you want to pursue this relationship, you really mean it.

SAGITTARIUS & AQUARIUS (JAN. 20–FEB. 18)

You are an idealist, but you do like to put your ideas into practical action. You're inspired by Aquarians, with their futuristic, lean, eclectic inventiveness and intuitive, brilliant out-of-the-box approach to life. Your Aquarius lover is most certainly a unique individual. With them, you feel like your life adventure is on the cutting edge of culture. This is a partnership of air mixed with fire. Aquarians fan the flames of your big ideas with unusual excitement of their own. The two of you can be terrific friends even if it doesn't become hot romantically. If you do choose to live together, a lack of daily routine can make it difficult to plant your feet firmly on the ground. Together, yours is an intellectual world of ideas, even if you tend to be more physical. Your partner must be willing to engage in the big outdoors and the physical aspects of love or you'll lose interest pretty quickly. If your Venus is in Scorpio, your emotional intensity may be at odds with your lover's easy sense of detachment, but with your Moon in an air sign, compatibility is increased. You stimulate each other and enhance each another's intuitive flashes of brilliance. You are a progressive duo and will likely enjoy making each and every moment count.

SAGITTARIUS & PISCES (FEB. 19–MARCH 20)

Archers are often interested in religious studies, philosophies, and global issues. You seek to create a path in life that balances your humanistic and individual goals. Pisces folks are also spiritually inclined, but are interested in the actual practices of religions, for they like to experience altered states brought on through spiritual practice. Or, they may just be attracted to fantasy. Either way, this is a rich relationship that will expand your horizons. Your Pisces lover seeks union with those who are able to perceive the mystical origins of life, and are drawn to those with charitable compassion. You share a mutual awareness of the world and a desire to aid those in need. Yet there are important differences in style. Your fiery nature is intellectual and action-oriented. Your water mate is less outgoing than you, and seeks emotional empathy. If you're able to allow for your differences, you will discover strength in this union, especially if you find a common cause. You'll need to pay attention to the sensitive needs of your Pisces lover and open your door to a world of rich imagination. He or she will have to be more active and adventurous. If you have Venus in Scorpio or the Moon in any water sign, compatibility is easier.

ABOUT THE AUTHORS

RICK LEVINE When I first encountered astrology as a psychology undergraduate in the late 1960s, I became fascinated with the varieties of human experience. Even now, I love the one-on-one work of seeing clients and looking at their lives through the cosmic lens. But I also love history and utilize astrology to better understand the longer-term cycles of cultural change. My recent DVD, *Quantum Astrology*, explores some of these transpersonal interests. As a scientist, I'm always looking for patterns in order to improve my ability to predict the outcome of any experiment; as an artist, I'm entranced by the mystery of what we do not and cannot know. As an astrologer, I am privileged to live in an enchanted world that links the rational and magical, physical and spiritual—and yes—even science and art.

JEFF JAWER I'm a Taurus with a Scorpio Moon and Aries rising who lives in the Pacific Northwest with Danick, my double-Pisces musician wife, our two Leo daughters, a black Gemini cat, and a white Pisces dog. I have been a professional astrologer since 1973 when I was a student at the University of Massachusetts (Amherst). I encountered astrology as my first marriage was ending and I was searching for answers. Astrology provided them. More than thirty-five years later, it remains the creative passion of my life as I continue to counsel, write, study, and share ideas with clients and colleagues around the world.

ACKNOWLEDGMENTS

Thanks to Paul O'Brien, our agent, our friend, and the creative genius behind Tarot.com; Gail Goldberg, the editor who always makes us sound better; Marcus Leaver and Michael Fragnito at Sterling Publishing, for their tireless support for the project; Barbara Berger, our supervising editor, who has shepherded this book with Taurean persistence and Aquarian invention; Laura Jorstad, for her refinement of the text; and Sterling project editor Mary Hern, assistant editor Sasha Tropp, and designer Abrah Griggs for their invaluable help. We thank Bob Wietrak and Jules Herbert at Barnes & Noble, and all of the helping hands at Sterling. Thanks for the art and ideas from Jessica Abel and the rest of the Tarot.com team. Thanks as well to 3+Co. for the original design and to Tara Gimmer for the author photo.